What the Experts are Saying about
Aligned

In *Aligned*, Maurice R. Parisien has written an engaging book about successful sales and marketing methods that uses an unusual technique: a conversational method showing how individual people approach marketing—making mistakes and correcting them. Reading like a novel, in *Aligned*, Parisien teaches modern successful marketing tactics in a refreshing way. Anyone who wants to learn about effective sales and marketing could not go wrong by reading this book.

ARTHUR MIDDLETON HUGHES
VP The Database Marketing Institute, Ltd.
author of six best selling marketing books including
Strategic Database Marketing 3rd Edition (McGraw-Hill 2006)

Successful instructors and writers know that context is necessary for a novice to learn and master complex new topics. One of the best methods to supply that context is through fictional narrative. In his book *Aligned*, Maurice Parisien uses experiential narrative to introduce marketing strategies and tactics in an engaging and understandable way. His approach provides an excellent platform to introduce basic concepts to an audience with no previous marketing experience. *Aligned* should be on the reading list of any entrepreneur starting a business where sales and marketing will drive success.

GARY FORD
Assistant Professor and Director of Graduate Studies,
School of Communications
Webster University, St. Louis, Missouri

When you get down in the trenches of business with Maurice Parisien, be prepared for learning things in a different way. It's a given that he has the expertise in the field of aligning marketing and sales, a challenge to many businesses under the best of circumstances. Add to this expertise his penchant for presenting and educating through story telling and you have an unbeatable one-two punch. Anyone who's ever struggled with starting or building a business will find serious help in the pages of *Aligned*.

DON KORNBLET
business owner and author,
Business Success Secrets

In the tradition of Patrick Lencioni, Maurice has crafted in *Aligned* a business book that is fun to read—a "page turner" that will benefit both those on the agency and client side of the table. He addresses the problems that are all too common in many businesses: the alignment of marketing and sales goals—in fact, the creation of meaningful marketing and sales goals—are all too often out of synch or undefined. His unique approach takes the growth challenge of a client and shows us the inner workings of two marketing services firms who vie for the prize. This is a business book worth the time to read and one that keeps you excited as it subliminally makes you take a hard look at your own company as you read.

WARREN A. HUNTER
Chairman & CEO
DMW Worldwide LLC

Aligned is an engaging tale of two marketing services agencies—one enlightened, one "old school." With a plot that unfolds like a novel, the reader is treated to insightful business analysis delivered with a user-friendly, approachable style. After just a few page turns, you feel like you personally know the lead characters and are emotionally connected with their business situations. You realize that what on the surface seems like an engaging storyline has actually been quite instructive in demonstrating the value of alignment. The book also sheds light on the emotional toll situations and decisions exact on business owners faced with difficult, real-world challenges. Importantly, it offers a methodical road map to success, based on the principles of alignment.

Aligned is a rare find among business books that takes the reader on a journey that is not just instructive in the value of aligning marketing and sales but is also captivating in its style.

MARY M. DEAN
Vice President, Innovation
Nestle Purina PetCare Company

The art of writing a great book requires the unique ability to tell a story, and in *Aligned* Maurice Parisien demonstrates his ability to do just that. *Aligned* follows the journey of two organizations that are driving toward the same goal, but with very different results. Throughout *Aligned,* Mr. Parisien brings the reader into the story to the point where he lives through every decision and outcome feeling both the highs and lows of each fateful step forward that the story takes.

When you read *Aligned* you're immediately compelled to think about your own organization, its vision, strategy and execution. *Aligned* is a must read for any business leader.

MARK SHIPLEY
Vice President, Loyalty Marketing
Sears Holdings Corporation

Alignment of sales and marketing has been elusive since Albert D. Lasker cranked up the marketing machine a hundred years ago. This is an easy to read, fictionalized account of a struggling company which is an exact copy of millions of businesses that exist today; the problems Parisien outlines are their problems. Companies that succeed in spite of their nonexistent sales and marketing alignment do so at the cost of slower growth and lower profitability. The ten chapters in this book tackle the evasively obvious issues that are easier to solve with his roadmap. There are take-aways at the end of each chapter and reproducible charts and graphs which you can actually understand. I like how he hammers on marketing ROI and sales accountability.

- Ideal for new marketers
- A must read for startup company presidents
- A necessity for larger companies that complain about sales and marketing's lack of alignment but fail to fix it.
- Agencies, whether branding, direct, or one of the many Internet agencies, should read this. I mean seriously read it.

JAMES W. OBERMAYER
Executive Director
Sales Lead Management Association

ALIGNED!

A Story for Improving Sales and Marketing Effectiveness

Maurice R. Parisien

Copyright © 2012 by Racom Communications

Published by
Racom Communications
150 N. Michigan Ave.
Suite 2800
Chicago, IL 60601
800-247-6553
www.racombooks.com

Editor: Richard Hagle

All rights reserved. No part of this book may be reproduced, stored in a retrieval system, or transmitted in any form or by any means, electric, mechanical, photocopying, recording, or otherwise, without the prior written permission of the publisher.

Catalog-in-Publication information available from the Library of Congress.

Cover design by Richard Hutnick and DH Creative Communications.

Printed in the United States of America

ISBN: 978-1-933199-38-2

*Dedicated to my supportive and loving wife, Joy,
and my two daughters, Katie and Molly,
who have taught me one of the most important lessons in life . . .
that with love of family and faith, all things are possible.*

Contents

Acknowledgments	vii
Foreword	ix
Prologue	xi
CHAPTER 1 Advanced Technologies	1
CHAPTER 2 The World According to MarCom Solutions	13
CHAPTER 3 The World According to GroupOne	23
CHAPTER 4 Advanced Technologies Meets MarCom Solutions	32
CHAPTER 5 Enter GroupOne	42
CHAPTER 6 AT's Customer Buying Process	51
CHAPTER 7 The Perfect Selling Process	60
CHAPTER 8 The Sales and Marketing Alignment Process	70
CHAPTER 9 Narrowing the Field	80
CHAPTER 10 MarCom Solutions versus GroupOne	92
EPILOGUE	103
APPENDIX	
Elements of Sales and Marketing Alignment	105
Sales and Marketing Alignment Continuum	106
Suggested Reading	110
Index	111

Acknowledgments

When I set out on the journey to write this, my first book, I began with a desire to write a book that would provide both insight and practical tools for marketers, sales managers, and business executives to be able to put into practice process changes that would ultimately improve marketing and sales effectiveness through greater alignment. As one who has spent his entire career working in both sales and marketing, from both sides of the desk, I've come to understand and learn firsthand the positive outcomes that can occur when proper alignment of sales and marketing is achieved. Therefore, I first want to acknowledge my first employer, Nestle Purina PetCare Company (at the time of my employment, Ralston Purina Company). My 14-year tenure with Ralston Purina formed a foundation of knowledge that enabled me to recognize the value that each of the disciplines of sales and marketing bring to the table and how great things can happen when sales and marketing work well together. In addition, I acknowledge the many clients, both large and small (and some in between), that I've had the privilege to work with over the years. These companies invited me into their organizations to help achieve their respective marketing/business goals through strategic, tactical, as well as process improvement initiatives.

When it comes to the composition of this book, I want to express a very special thanks to Arthur Hughes, a true gentleman, renowned author, database marketing educator and practitioner, who has inspired me over the past twenty years to pursue a career that has brought much satisfaction and fulfillment. What's more, beyond coming up with the concept for a new book and stepping out to put those very first words to paper, without the help of my editor and publisher, my work would never have come to see the light of day. So for this, I offer my deepest gratitude to my editor, Seth Thompson, his constant encouragement, his eye for quality prose and his commitment to providing the polish necessary to make for a book that not only contains valuable content, but also is a pleasure to read. And to my publisher, Racom Communications and Rich Hagle, who could see the value in my manuscript and was willing to take the risk of bringing this work to life. And finally, to my friends, family members and close business associates who provided encouragement every step of the way in the writing and pursuit of publishing, each of you have my sincere gratitude. *Now on with the story . . .*

Foreword

In this unusual book, Maurice Parisien takes the reader through the process of choosing an agency to help a company with its advertising and sales. In conversational tones Maurice explores the benefits of two agencies, developing a useful scoring system for rating them. Most large companies have to make this decision at some time. Few have the time or the experience to develop a comprehensive selection system comparable to what Maurice provides in this book. Before they start the process, they should read this book.

One important point that Maurice focuses on is the differing approaches of marketing and sales. In my working life, I have worked for both disciplines. I know that marketing often develops expensive creative pieces that, in fact, are not of much use to the sales staff. Some sales members look down on marketing, saying, "They talk a good game, but they have never closed a sale. That is what we do." Some marketing executives look down on sales, saying "Sales is based on an 'old boy network.' Their materials look cheap—they will never win an 'Echo Award' with the junk they turn out."

This difference was illustrated in a chapter in my third marketing book, *The Complete Database Marketer* Revised Edition (McGraw-Hill, 1996) in which I wrote: "Why Salespeople Fight Marketing Databases":

> A marketing database implies direct sales, which means that no salespeople will be needed. Sales will be cut out of the loop and the commissions. Salespeople are usually asked to provide the database with a list of their contacts. Salespeople live by their contacts. To surrender them is to give up their livelihood. Once the names are in the database you will write letters to them and call them; the next thing you know, your telemarketers will be selling to them, not the salesman. Goodbye, commissions. . . .
>
> Look at it from the salespeople's point of view. They are out on the firing line, trying to find leads, win them over, make sales and get commissions. Marketing people think that they can do the same thing by direct mail and telemarketing. This is threatening. Suppose they are correct? They will force salespeople out of their jobs. Even if the marketers are not correct, they will waste a lot of time, get credit for half of the sales and cut into salespeople's opportunities to make commissions. What good can possibly come out of cooperating with them?
>
> To top it off, marketing departments are often staffed by MBAs who have learned all the theory, but have never, in fact, closed on a sale themselves. They consider themselves above the crass business of asking for a sale. They want to conduct marketing with computers, producing reams of fine reports and statistics.

You may smile at these differences, but they are real differences in most companies, and unless you recognize the problems and deal with them your marketing database will be a failure.

Janet Park, President of Marketing Frontiers, tells an interesting story which illustrates this point. I was having lunch one day with several executives from a leading business-to-business list compiler. They were describing to me in detail the intricacies of their three-year database research project for one of the largest and most sophisticated marketing companies in the United States. Millions of dollars had been spent on surveys, data overlays and analytical models to refine the perfect business list for supporting their brokers in the field offices. "That same afternoon, I had a meeting with a friend of mine who just happened to be a broker for the same sophisticated marketing company mentioned above. I asked him how he got his leads. 'Yellow Pages,' he said. 'I look in the Yellow Pages and call them up. Sometimes,' he added guiltily, 'I just resort to smokestacking. If I see an interesting looking building while driving around, I'll just stop and make a cold call to see if there's anything worth pursuing.'

With *ALIGNED* you rise above these differences and use a sophisticated scoring system to make your decision in selecting an agency. Well worth reading.

ARTHUR MIDDLETON HUGHES
Vice President, The Database Marketing Institute
April 15, 2011

Prologue

A wise businessperson once said that nothing happens in business until someone sells something. Well, that is true, but you can't sell something without first understanding your sales target. How efficiently a company responds to customer needs predicts success or failure in sales and marketing. Nevertheless, many sales and marketing teams remain at conceptual odds in they how promote products and services to new and existing customers. In the business-to-business arena, successful companies separate themselves from the pack in two major ways: by clearly understanding *why* customers are buying and then linking the sales process with *how* customers are buying.

This book reveals the importance of this relationship by telling the story of two marketing agencies as they assist clients with product marketing. The first company, MarCom Solutions, develops creative messaging and promotional offers for their clients' well-defined prospect universe, while the second company, GroupOne, effectively aligns their clients' sales and marketing teams, demonstrating the value of synergy in sales and marketing. Although fictional accounts of real business world dilemmas, these stories faithfully chronicle how many companies fail or succeed in their efforts to grow business by either ignoring the need for alignment in sales and marketing, or recognizing and embracing its ability to deliver measurable top-line growth.

Stories of sales and marketing are unique in that, on a macro level, they contain only protagonists. Companies working for measurable business growth do not struggle upstream against meddlesome forces. Instead, they race downstream with the competition towards the next gulf of opportunity, and whoever has the fastest canoe (i.e., the most integrated sales and marketing process) gets there first. In today's fast-paced business environment, meeting client needs without first having to address your own sales and marketing practices is imperative to staying ahead of the pack.

Oscar Wilde once quipped: "Nothing succeeds like success." Concerning sales and marketing, he was right. A successful sales and marketing process leads to a successful business, and proper alignment in sales and marketing leads to a successful sales and marketing process. Whether you work for a marketing agency, are a business/marketing student, or are considering hiring consultants to help propel your business into the future, the stories in this book take you out of academia and into the real business world to help you make everyday sales and marketing decisions that insure success, that you might accomplish your goal of "selling something," and continue to make your business "happen."

1
Advanced Technologies

Husband and wife business team Frank and Marlie Scott founded Advanced Technologies in June 2005. A software development firm better known as "AT," their company saw decent profits in its first six months from one-off sales of software that quickly became obsolete, but Frank, the firm's creative side, had been developing a unique security program that allowed companies to decide who accessed their proprietary data files. By January 2006, it was trademarked, patented and ready to market under the brand name SecureSoft, fulfilling the business plan that Marlie, the firm's technical guru, had devised at the program's inception.

Over the next year and a half, several companies showed interest in SecureSoft, but no one stepped up to make a purchase. AT's primary business challenge was becoming evident: In order to sell SecureSoft, it needed to address some basic marketing issues. With their hopefulness degenerating to hand wringing, Frank and Marlie asked themselves a series of tough questions:

- How commercially viable is SecureSoft?
- What is its unique value proposition?
- What problem(s) does it solve?
- Who are its ideal customers and why would they buy it?

Like many software companies, AT had created some impressive technology, but it seemed to be a solution in search of a problem. The Scotts had planned to celebrate SecureSoft's first sale within 6 months of its release, but after the passage of 18 months that felt like 18 years, the champagne still chilled in the cellar. The company was able to make payroll, but their bench of software developers was growing impatient, grumbling among themselves that SecureSoft was a failure and that brighter pastures lay elsewhere.

Recognizing that their situation was more of a marketing dilemma than anything else, Frank and Marlie decided to seek the assistance of a marketing consultant, someone who could help them sort through their sales and marketing issues and come up with a strategic marketing plan to make their product succeed. With cash running thin, they needed a consultant who was willing to take a portion of his or her payment as equity in AT. After several dismal interviews, they discovered Joe Albright, a reputable sales and marketing consultant with more than twenty years' experience. He was well tailored, well groomed, and well educated, having graduated near the top of his class at Truman State and having received his MBA from Northwestern. Over the past fourteen years, he had worked for two companies, spending the first eight as a marketing manager for a casket company and the last six as VP of Sales and Marketing for a Fortune 500 healthcare provider. He was professional yet personable, and, given his training and experience, he was precisely what AT needed.

The first step for Joe, Frank, and Marlie was to carve out two full days to begin AT's strategic planning for SecureSoft. When AT was formed, Marlie had written a detailed business plan, but that was two years ago, and neither she nor Frank had revisited it. Before AT could move forward, it needed a map that put it on a path to success. The date for the strategic planning session was set. Joe and the Scotts would meet in two weeks at a nearby hotel after each of them had fulfilled a certain task. Joe would gather industry data and Frank would study competitors, while Marlie collected AT's financial and performance data. The Scotts sensed that they were on the right path and passed the two weeks in guarded excitement.

On September 18, they met Joe at 8:00 A.M. in one of the hotel's conference rooms. It had the feel of a physician's waiting room. Its starving artist paintings, teal wallpaper, and corporate furniture gave off an air of manufactured warmth, but after a continental breakfast of powdered donuts and fresh coffee, the group kicked off their planning session with brio. Joe, having led such planning sessions before, knew what he was doing. He began with a SWOT (Strengths, Weaknesses, Opportunities & Threats) analysis, which yielded a long list of AT's strengths that was pared down to the following:

STRENGTHS
- Unique technology.
- Bright and capable employees.
- Technology that addresses a "real" need.
- Positive response from prospective clients.

Then the team approached the other three dimensions of the SWOT analysis and came up with the following characteristics:

WEAKNESSES
- No customers after 18 months.
- Low on cash.
- No prospect database in place.
- No bench program to fill the void if current program fails to catch on.

OPPORTUNITIES
- Consider traditional advertising and direct marketing strategies.
- Define AT's Unique Value Proposition.
- Leverage PR and Speaking engagements.
- Identify markets/industry sectors that would value AT's solution.

THREATS
- Shifting economy may cause prospective clients to avoid investing in new software.
- A major software developer has been investigating the opportunity in AT's software solution space.
- Competition is heating up in the space.
- AT's software developers are displeased with the current sales situation and may pursue other opportunities.

After two and a half hours of concerted effort, the team needed a break. Joe left the room to check his email while Frank and Marlie stayed behind to revisit the SWOT analysis.

Marlie turned to Frank. "Do we really have what it takes to make this happen?"

"What are you saying?" Frank winced.

"We've been at this for two years and I just wonder if. . . . "

"We can't quit now," interrupted Frank.

Marlie shot him an incredulous look. "I'm not suggesting we quit, but look at the hurdles we have to jump."

"Yes, but look at all the positive things we have going for us," he interjected. "Look at the strengths we put on the board. We've *got* what it takes."

"I agree with you, Frank. I'm just concerned. We're running out of cash, and if we don't make a sale soon, we're either going to need investors, who won't be easy to find right now, or we'll have to mortgage the house, and I'm not too keen on another mortgage."

Joe reentered the conference room and sensed discussion had taken place. "Marlie, how are you feeling at this point in the process?" Joe began.

"Well, Joe, I gotta tell you, I'm concerned. The SWOT exercise was helpful, but it makes me wonder whether we're going to be able to pull ourselves out of this slump and turn this business around."

Joe turned to Frank. "What's your take on where we're at?"

"I understand Marlie's concerns. They're well founded," Frank remarked. "But I believe that we can work our way through this. Yes, we have challenges, but they're basically sales and marketing challenges, which is why you're here."

"Thanks for the vote of confidence," Joe joked.

"I think we should spend more time discussing the value points of our product, because I don't think we've properly defined its unique value proposition," Frank said. "What do you guys think?"

Marlie and Joe agreed, with Joe suggesting that they elucidate SecureSoft's unique characteristics. "Let's take some time to define the program's characteristics, and then we'll match them with their benefits." Frank and Marlie agreed and decided on the following characteristics:

PRODUCT CHARACTERISTICS
- Ability to prevent data from being repurposed in any form.
- Allows only designated users to access proprietary data.
- Tracks when and how data is accessed with a user "thumb print."
- Allows authorized users to change size and font to fit needs.
- Compatible with any browser.

Then Joe suggested contemplating SecureSoft from a user perspective by discussing how users would benefit from the application:

PRODUCT BENEFITS
- Prevents valuable content from falling into unauthorized hands.
- Will save companies millions of dollars by securing proprietary data.
- Provides a "digital trail" for quick and accurate tracing of data files.
- Ability to personalize the look and feel of documents.
- Application works with any browser.

After documenting the associated features and benefits of SecureSoft, the team broke for lunch, where they decided their next step should be to devise an effective pricing plan for SecureSoft. As they finished their ham sandwiches and chips, Joe advised that the best approach was to price SecureSoft as a SaaS (software as a service) offering, with Frank and Marlie deciding to price it based on the number of "potential users" who could access proprietary documents. To keep things simple, they would price SecureSoft at three levels. The first, or "smallbiz," level would be for companies of fewer than 150 employees, while the second, "mid-tier" level would apply to companies of between 151 and 2,000 employees. Finally, the third, "enterprise" level would be for companies of 2,001 or more employees.

When SecureSoft hit the market the Scotts decided on a set price for the entire program. The problem with this pricing model was that it was too expensive for smaller companies yet not priced high enough for larger enterprise accounts. Furthermore, a one-off sales approach did not provide a way to up-sell a customer as new program features became available. With the pricing discussion behind them, the team set about establishing some reasonable sales goals for the next 6 to 12 months.

Joe estimated SecureSoft's sales cycle would be roughly 90 days. It was a complex sale involving a number of management personnel in the buying decision, and the significant money value of the sale would influence the length of the cycle as well. Even though AT had put together a compelling business case to sell-in Secure-

Soft, a $36,000 annual renewable investment would still be prohibitive for most companies, especially if the expenditure was not budgeted. After carefully considering the customer buying process at all account levels, the team arrived at a realistic sales budget. To be conservative, sales for the next 12 months were set at $1 million with plans to double the business in the second 12 months and then double it again a year later. Assuming that SecureSoft met its new customer acquisition targets for the next three years and retained three-fourths of them, AT would be a $4 million a year business in its third year.

At 5:00 P.M., Joe and the Scotts ended their first day of strategic planning. They had accomplished a lot and agreed that they would reconvene at 8:00 A.M. the following morning. On the drive home, Frank and Marlie reflected on the day.

"So, what's your overall impression of how things went today," Frank started.

"I don't know. I have mixed feelings," Marlie replied.

"What do you mean?" asked Frank.

"Well, I'm excited about getting this business off the ground, but we have so much work to do on our own sales and marketing, and neither one of us really has the skills to do it. I think it would be wise for us to spend some time thinking about what we're going to need to have a sales and marketing plan that works for *us* instead of us having to work for *it*."

Frank agreed. "I think you hit the nail on the head. Part of the reason we haven't been successful is because we lack sales and marketing experience. So, let's talk to Joe about this first thing in the morning. It'll be time well spent. But, right now, I think stopping at our favorite restaurant for dinner and a good bottle of wine would be time well spent. You up for it?"

Marlie didn't hesitate. "Ah, our favorite haunt. You bet. I'll call and see if we need reservations."

The next morning, the group showed up early and got their meeting underway 8:00 A.M. sharp. Frank spoke first. "Joe, Marlie and I were reflecting on our meeting yesterday and thought that we should spend some time this morning thinking through the sales and marketing issues that we need to address to be able to accomplish the goals we've set. Since Marlie and I lack the skills and experience to successfully market our product, I think we need to clearly define the sales and marketing process so we can understand exactly what it takes to align our sales and marketing approaches."

Joe was pleased that Frank and Marlie were coming together on this critical point of strategic insight.

"Frank, I couldn't agree with you more," Joe responded. "If I may, let me share with you something that I've told C-level executives in both my consulting and speaking engagements."

Joe approached a dry erase board with marker in hand. "You see, sales and marketing teams often stand at odds in terms of how they develop a plan versus how they carry it out. You'll commonly find marketing departments analyzing market opportunities, developing brand strategies, and creating tactical communications materials for the sales force, while the sales force is on the street trying to drum up business. What I've found to be most effective is when sales and marketing teams come together and share the responsibility of acquiring, growing, and retaining customers."

Joe drew two triangles on the board in the manner seen in Exhibit 1-1. At the top of the inverted pyramid, Joe wrote the word "Marketing" and then wrote the word "Sales" at the base of the upright pyramid. Then he explained the theory of sales and marketing alignment.

Exhibit 1-1

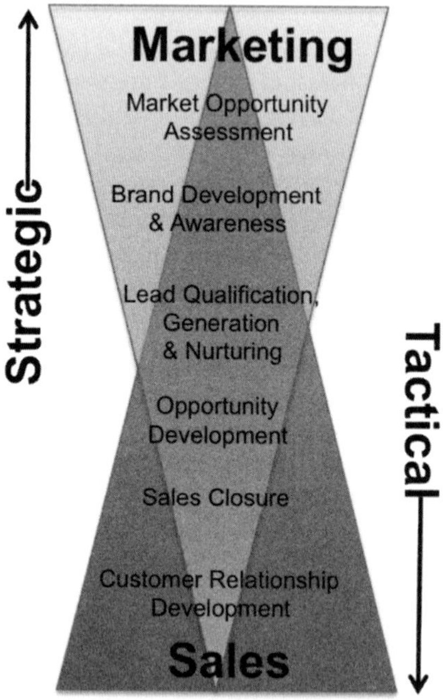

Marketing
- Market Opportunity Assessment
- Brand Development & Awareness
- Lead Qualification, Generation & Nurturing
- Opportunity Development
- Sales Closure
- Customer Relationship Development

Sales

Strategic ↕ Tactical

"If you conceive of sales and marketing as two disciplines that work together to create a customer acquisition and development engine, you arrive at the common area of these two pyramids where, after marketing takes primary responsibility for *market opportunity assessment* and sales does the same for *customer relationship development*, their respective efforts should become intertwined. As you can see, when we get to *lead qualification, generation and nurturing*, it's as if sales and marketing share equally in the work, because even though a marketing team is delivering and nurturing leads that aren't yet 'sales ready,' the sales team should be helping the marketing team define qualified leads. I call this point in the process the 'tipping point.' If a sales team doesn't accurately define the characteristics of a qualified lead to a marketing team and a marketing team doesn't internalize the definition in order to provide qualified leads to sales, then the whole the system breaks down; and from that point forward, marketing and sales essentially fail to capitalize on each other's skills and abilities, creating operational inefficiency that wastes time and money. But if the system runs properly, the quality, quantity, and timeliness of leads is addressed by both sales and marketing. If sales and marketing do their jobs well, they continuously assess the customer's needs and deliver solutions that are valuable to the customer and profitable to the enterprise. Does this make sense?"

"Perfect sense," the Scotts replied almost in unison.

"So," began Frank, "if we adopt this model, we need to think through the sub-process elements for each of the major process steps and . . . "

"That won't be an issue," Joe cut in. "I've already developed the detailed processes that fall under each of these major process elements."

"Okay," Frank replied, "but we need to think about the people requirements as well. We need to identify the human resources that we'll need to manage a fully integrated marketing and sales process."

"You're right, Frank," Joe replied, "but I don't think that your company will have to take all of that on by itself; at least, not if you're comfortable with outsourcing. We should think about the expertise that you would need to manage the overall process, as well as execute certain elements of it."

"I'm not sure I'm clear on where you're heading with this," Frank said.

"Well," Joe continued, "I think that, if you hired a sales executive with experience in marketing and high level, complex B2B sales, you could outsource your marketing requirements. The key will be finding a partner who has worked with organizations that have created alignment between sales and marketing."

"I don't know, Joe," Frank remarked. "That sounds like a pretty tall order."

"I didn't say it would be easy, but I've worked with some forward-thinking marketing firms that have helped clients achieve impressive top-line growth while delivering an impressive ROI."

Marlie was quietly absorbing Frank and Joe's discussion, when she suddenly spoke up. "What if we spent some time documenting the requirements of both the sales executive and the marketing firm. If we were able to knock that out today, we'd be able to take some immediate steps towards our search for a sales executive, as well as the marketing services company. What do you think?"

"Let's do it," said Frank. "Great idea, Marlie," Joe replied. "Whatever path you decide to take with outsourcing, this is something that we're going to need to knock out sooner or later."

Then Joe turned to defining the characteristics of the ideal sales executive and the ideal marketing firm.

Joe reviewed the characteristics of the ideal sales executive and the ideal marketing services firm. "Do you think we missed anything?" he asked the Scotts.

"No, I think we've covered all the bases," Frank said.

"What do you think, Marlie?" Joe continued.

"At the very least, this is a good head start," she replied.

It was mid-afternoon, and the team was anxious to detail a plan of action that would begin moving AT forward. Joe thought that they should summarize everything

Exhibit 1-2

Sales Executive	Marketing Firm
Seven to ten yrs experience with B2B companies	Proven performance in developing and executing demand generation programs for B2B companies
Four yr. college degree, MBA a plus	Senior agency members engaged in the assignment
Experience selling-in at the C suite	Services priced to deliver an ROI that exceeds 300% within six months
Experience selling intangibles	Willingness to base a portion of fees on performance
Proven performer in complex five to six figure sales	Good bench strength in program strategy, tactics and analytics
Ability to pass a third party administered assessment process	Experience aligning sales and marketing teams

they had covered in their two sessions and then compose a list of action items, assigning responsibilities and time lines to each one.

"Before we put together an action list and assign responsibilities and dates, I think it would be helpful to recap what we've covered thus far," said Joe, with Frank and Marlie nodding agreement.

Referring to the SWOT analysis (Exhibit 1-3), the team reviewed the following Strengths, Weaknesses, Opportunities and Threats facing AT in relation to SecureSoft.

Next, the team revisited SecureSoft's characteristics and their associated benefits (Exhibit 1-4).

Then the team decided to address one of the "opportunities" that was identified in the SWOT analysis: developing a unique value proposition (UVP) for SecureSoft. Joe's framework for constructing the UVP consisted of three simple elements:

1. **Brand Strength:** A statement of the product's characteristics.
2. **Linkage:** The resulting benefit of using the product.
3. **End Benefits:** The product's unique impact that shows the product's superiority to similar products.

Exhibit 1-3

Strengths	Weaknesses
Unique technology	No customers after 18 months
Bright and capable employees	Low on cash
Technology addresses a "real" need	No prospect database in place
Positive response form prospective clients	No bench program to fill the void if current program fails to catch on.
Opportunities	**Threats**
Consider traditional advertising and direct marketing strategies	Shifting economy may cause prospective clients to avoid buying new software
Define AT's unique value proposition	Another software developer is seeking opportunity in AT's software solution space
Leverage PR and Speaking engagements	Competition is heating up in the space
Identify markets/industry sectors that would value AT's new program	AT's software developers are displeased with the current sales situation and may pursue other opportunities

Exhibit 1-4

Characteristics	Benefits
Ability to prevent data from being re-purposed in any way	Protects valuable content from falling into unauthorized hands
Allows only designated users to access proprietary data	Will save companies millions of dollars by securing proprietary data.
Tracks when and how data is accessed with a user "thumb print"	Provides a secure "digital-trail" for quick and accurate tracing of data files.
Allows authorized users to change font and size to fit needs	Ability to personalize the "look" and "feel" of documents
Compatible with any browser	Application works with any browser

Using these elements as a framework, the team drafted SecureSoft's UVP:

> SecureSoft is a browser-based application that secures digital content (audio, video, text) by allowing foreign entities to access such content on a permission only basis. SecureSoft possesses the unique capability to deliver the appropriate level of data security to a wide range of users, resulting in a solution that protects valuable content from falling into unauthorized hands. In addition, SecureSoft provides a secure "digital-thumbprint" and an easy to trace data trail for all accessed files. SecureSoft saves companies millions of dollars annually by protecting them from the unauthorized access, use and re-purposing of their proprietary data.

In wrapping up the activities for day two of AT's strategic planning session, Joe assigned the following tasks with a timeframe for each one (Exhibit 1-5).

Exhibit 1-5

Task	Responsibility	Days from Today
Initiate search for sales executive	Frank	2 days
Identify a minimum of three sales executive candidates	Frank & Recruiter	30 days
Complete selection assessments for candidate(s)	Frank & HR consultant	45 days
Hire sales executive	Frank & Marlie	50 days
Complete draft #1 of the sales and marketing plan	Joe	10 days
Initiate search for marketing services agencies	Joe	2 days
Presentations of agency capabilities	Frank, Marlie & Joe	30 days
Formal statement of requirements to agencies on the short list	Joe	35 days
Review agency responses	Frank, Marlie & Joe	50 days
Select agency	Frank, Marlie, Joe and new sales executive	55 days

Key Takeaways from Chapter 1

The first step in increasing a business's profitability is to step back and take a hard look at the systems, processes and resources that support the disciplines of sales and marketing. In AT's case, the Scotts recognized that they lacked the requisite skills and experience to put together a great sales and marketing plan, so they turned an experienced sales and marketing consultant to walk with them through the process. Additionally, the Scotts realized that they lacked the expertise and experience of a sales professional that could identify customer needs that would be satisfied by SecureSoft.

As committed as AT was to succeeding with SecureSoft, the Scotts needed to take a hard look at the marketplace and the value that SecureSoft brought to the market. Just because some bright developers were able to build a great product did not mean that people were ready to buy the product. Beyond their initial planning meeting, the Scotts would need to conduct qualitative and quantitative market research to assess which industry verticals would be most likely to purchase SecureSoft. A sales and marketing plan would then be grounded in a realistic sales forecast. With an educated expectation of first-year sales, a well-conceived sales plan could then be employed (e.g., direct sales, distributors, brokers, inside sales, etc.) to meet the business goals. Hand in hand with the sales plan would be a marketing plan that generated qualified leads to secure new customers. Successful B2B companies find that using fully integrated and automated demand generation systems maximizes their return on marketing investment (ROMI). A demand generation system is a multi-touch, multi-channel approach to generate awareness and qualified interest in the marketplace for a solution that addresses a real business need.

Early in the process, companies must focus on identifying the key metrics or key performance indicators (KPIs) of the sales and marketing process. As the name implies, KPIs represent the ultimate criteria by which management and staff monitor performance throughout the sales and marketing process to assess sales and marketing effectiveness. Beyond unit sales and dollar sales, the management of a company would be well served to consider the following metrics in determining how to improve the sales and marketing process:

- Qualified leads in the pipeline
- Lead quality by lead source
- Value and quantity of leads at each step in the sales process
- Ratio of leads to closed business
- Average length of the sales cycle in days
- Marketing spend by tactic
- Sales by tactic

In the end, an integrated sales and marketing plan will lead to business success. However, success will come only to companies that do a proper job of researching the market and properly executing their research-based sales and marketing plan.

The team had made major strides in its two days of planning, but more work lay ahead. The good news was that a path to success had been set and each of the team members were eager to embark upon it.

"Joe, we've had a great two days," said Frank. "I have to tell you, we couldn't have done it without you. Do you have time for a drink?"

Marlie was standing near and heard the invitation. "Aren't I invited?"

Frank smiled at Marlie, and then turned back to Joe. "Come on, let's all pack up and head to Lorenzo's Bistro."

AT had taken its first major step in moving from being a company on the brink to a business with a potentially bright future. Although bright and talented, the Scotts did not possess the skills to plan and execute an effective sales and marketing plan, but Joe had stepped in to fill the void. With his coaching and counseling, AT was on the road to success.

2
The World According to MarCom Solutions

When MarCom Solutions opened its doors in 1985, its founders cut their teeth in the advertising and promotion business, focusing mainly on direct marketing/direct mail. Chief Creative Officer, Jeremy Miles, had an eye for quality graphics and a great headline. Stephen Collins was the agency's president. His strategic thinking skills combined with Jeremy's creativity to make them a formidable team. Over the years, they built a $15 million dollar agency. They had a handful of business-to-business accounts, but 80 percent of the agency's revenue came from large-volume consumer direct mail programs. In 2001, MarCom initiated the development of its Internet and e-marketing practice. Since then, the agency had successfully designed and executed numerous e-marketing campaigns for their clients, but the campaigns were never part of an integrated marketing communications strategy.

MarCom Solutions' Director of Client Services, Christine Marquette, was experienced, bright, and energetic. She earned her undergraduate degree from the University of New Hampshire and her MBA from Stephens College. MarCom was her first job out of college. She had been there for eight years, starting as an assistant account services manager and gradually working her way into her current position of three years.

The fourth member of MarCom's management team was the CFO, Mary Walker. An experienced financial manager, Mary joined the agency in 2003 after working for 10 years at one of the top-five accounting firms in the country, where she had grown weary of her workload. One day, she just happened to be contacted by a management recruitment firm. Two weeks later, she was interviewing with Jeremy and Stephen. She passed her interview with flying colors. It took Jeremy and Stephen only three weeks to extend Mary an offer. The compensation package included a slightly lower salary than she would have liked, but it was still more than what she was making in her current position. To sweeten the offer, MarCom included an attractive stock option package and a $5,000 signing bonus. It was enough for Mary to accept the offer and join the agency. Soon after joining Mar-

Com, she put a number of new financial controls in place. Of particular concern to Mary was MarCom's the lack of expense controls. In her first year, she was able to bring MarCom a six-figure cost savings that had a commensurate positive impact on the agency's bottom line.

The fifth member of MarCom's management team was VP of Sales, John Moloney. John had over 20 years of sales experience, but he had never held a managerial position that included people responsibility. Since he joined the company four years ago, MarCom had experienced modest growth, averaging a 3 percent year-over-year CAGR. John was a stereotypically gregarious salesperson, and while his business acumen was good, he was more tactical than strategic in his thinking. He led a sales team of seven people who varied in experience and expertise. The Pareto principle (80/20 rule) applied to MarCom's account base. The top sales rep, Bill Wright, produced twice the annual revenue of the average sales representative. In 2008, revenues from Bill's client list topped $5.4 million, delivering over 35 percent of the company's revenues.

When John joined the organization, management did not keep an accurate assessment of the sales pipeline, and they were generally unclear about where new business opportunities were positioned in the sales process. John held weekly sales meetings on Monday mornings, where each representative provided an update of his or her pipeline reports But the evaluation of the reports was highly subjective, leaving management unable to accurately forecast the timing and volume of pending sales.

Missing from MarCom's sales approach was a clearly defined and repeatable sales process. Every sales rep was left to his or her own devices in qualifying new opportunities, uncovering customer needs, nurturing the opportunities, and closing sales. Without an efficient sales process in place, opportunities were lost, and the average size of new deals was not as big as it should have been. Stephen and Mary had met with John on multiple occasions to discuss improving sales process and financial reporting, but little improvement happened. Finally, Stephen called a meeting one Friday to begin to put in place a formal sales process. The meeting was set for 2:00 P.M. and scheduled to last one hour.

Stephen and Mary got to the conference room first. John showed up five minutes late.

"Sorry I'm a few minutes late," John apologized. "The meeting invite wasn't clear. What's the purpose of the meeting?"

Stephen looked up from his notepad. "John, since you've been on board here, we've had numerous conversations where I've encouraged you to develop a sales process that's repeatable and fully transparent to management. For several months now, Christine has been concerned that the folks in operations are clueless about what's coming down the sales pipe, particularly when new opportunities are sold and projects are to be initiated. What can we do to move this initiative forward?"

John was surprised. Even though he and Stephen had spoken about improving MarCom's sales process, he had sensed that it was not one of Stephen's high priorities. "Well, Stephen, it's going to take considerable time and effort, and I'll probably need the assistance of a sales consultant. In other words, we'll have to make a financial commitment to document and reengineer our sales process."

"How much is it going to cost and what would be the timeline for implementation?" Stephen asked.

"I can't answer those questions right now, but if you give me time to check some resources, I can get back to you with a plan and a budget shortly," John replied.

"John, I'd be happy to help you check out some resources," said Mary.

"Thanks for the offer, Mary, but I should handle this one on my own."

"When can you get back to us with your thoughts on an approach, John?"

"How about two weeks?" John asked.

"How about one week from this coming Wednesday?" Stephen asked.

"Sounds good, Stephen. Is there anything else?"

"Not right now. We'll be anxious to see what you come up with."

"You bet, Stephen. You two have a great weekend."

With that, John left the room. Stephen and Mary stayed behind to discuss the matter further. Stephen turned to Mary. "What do you think of his response?"

"He appeared to be caught a little off guard," Mary replied, "but I would think that, given the number of conversations that you've had with him and the time that he and I have spent discussing the weaknesses in our current forecasting system, he would have come forward well before now with a solution to address the weaknesses in our sales forecasting system and the inconsistency in the sales process."

Stephen thought for a moment. "We'll see what he comes up with. I welcome your help in staying on top of this. If we're going to grow this business at the rate that we have in our current plan, we've got to get this stuff fixed. At any rate, we'll talk more on Monday. Have a good weekend, Mary."

"You too, Stephen."

MarCom did a poor job of marketing its own services. No one in management was responsible for overseeing the agency's marketing practices. Traditional B2B advertising and sales supportive marketing in the form of lead generation or demand generation/demand creation was nonexistent, which made sales representatives responsible for uncovering their own leads. MarCom had yet to recognize the value of employing a demand generation program as an effective means of acquiring new accounts. When a well-designed and executed demand generation program is in place, it delivers highly qualified prospects to the sales team that ultimately yield a high percentage of closed sales.

Another weakness in MarCom's marketing efforts was its poor web presence. There was no strategy to drive traffic to the site, which was probably a good thing, given its poor design and lack of meaningful content concerning MarCom's services. To make matters worse, the web site contained no case histories of business conducted with past clients, and no effort had been made to provide white papers in exchange for capturing visitor names and contact information. Although MarCom frequently advised its clients on the value of Internet marketing, it did little to leverage its own presence on the Internet.

Competing in creative award programs was the sole marketing strategy that Jeremy and Stephen had employed since MarCom began. MarCom competed annually in a local direct marketing awards competition and participated in a national awards competition semiannually. The agency would then mention its awards in marketing communications messages delivered by direct mail, email, and print advertising.

MarCom's challenges were not limited to the sales and marketing process, for the agency had done little to document its work processes. The operations team, headed by Christine Marquette, had a good handle on servicing clients once they came in the door, but the documentation of the servicing processes was neither current nor complete. Each of the account services managers used a documented process that had been in place since the agency was formed, but account managers would modify the process without documenting the improvements, communicating the changes by word-of-mouth to current employees. This lack of documentation made it difficult for new employees to learn the current process, resulting in a loss of productivity and process output, which resulted in a higher cost of service delivery. Christine was aware of the problem, but she had had little time to devote to its solution. She was hopeful that, at some point in the near future, she would be able to document the servicing process and then go back through its sub-processes to make process improvements that would enhance productivity and service quality.

Another of MarCom's shortcomings was its lack of a company vision statement. Jeremy and Stephen occasionally talked about defining the agency's mission, vision, and values, but it never went beyond a casual discussion. However, considering that MarCom's strategic plan had not been revisited since it was first drafted more than 20 years ago, MarCom's failure to define its vision was not surprising.

MarCom's client list was healthy with the majority of its clients coming from the telecommunications sector. The clients were largely mid-tier companies with a few Fortune 1000 companies thrown in the mix. The work for the Fortune 1000 clients subsisted in project-oriented assignments, while the mid-tier engagements tended to be long-term, retainer-based relationships. MarCom's average client relationship lasted between three and four years, although a few of the mid-tier agencies had been clients since MarCom began. MarCom's services tended to be tactical instead of strategic in nature. Most of MarCom's clients involved neither MarCom's management team nor their own in annual marketing planning events, and most of the client engagements took place by telephone. The client called one of Christine's account service representatives and requested a mailing to a segment of the client's "house file." New customer acquisition programs were the commonest of MarCom's tactical initiatives. The agency would first reach out to one of its list services partners to secure a mailing list, which resulted in a prospect file that addressed defined demographics to achieve a client's marketing goals. MarCom was weak on strategy and big on tactics.

On Monday morning, Stephen walked by John's desk to ask him how his weekend was.

"My weekend went well, Stephen. Thanks for asking. How was yours?"

"Great," Stephen replied. The weather couldn't have been better."

"I know," John replied. "My wife and I took a bike ride on Saturday."

Then Stephen brought the conversation around to business. "Have you given more thought to our discussion on Friday?"

"Yes, I have," replied John. "I'm going to be on the phone today with a couple of sales consultants I ran into at a recent sales conference. I figured they'd be a good place to start."

"Sounds good," Stephen responded. "You might also try an Internet search. I did a Google search over the weekend using the keywords "sales" and "process" and came up with six consulting firms."

"Yes, I'll be doing a Google search. I should have my research done by this Thursday, and I'll get my recommendations to you and Mary by next Wednesday. Is there anything else?"

"No, that's it," said Stephen.

"Great! Have a good day, Stephen."

"Thanks, John. You do the same."

John opened his computer browser, entered the keywords "sales" and "process" into a Google search and came up with 122 million references to the combined keywords. To narrow the results, he included the keyword "consulting," which yielded 432,000 references. On the first page of the search results, he immediately recognized the company name, Sales Leaders, LLC. The firm had been in business for thirty years and had worked with numerous companies in a number of industries. As he read the firm's web site, he saw that they had experience addressing most of the issues that MarCom was facing, including:

- Improving Sales Force Productivity.
- Better Managing Sales Talent.
- Shortening Sales Cycles.
- Improving Sales Forecasting Accuracy.

After looking over the company's web site, John sent Sales Leaders a brief email seeking a response to some of MarCom's particular needs. In the meantime, he researched other possible vendors and found the same issues addressed, with some consulting organizations creating their own lexicon concerning sales process and performance. Being a straight-talking sales pro who disliked corporate pitches that used a new vocabulary to describe age-old business issues, John immediately discounted these organizations. In the end, he decided to approach three consulting firms, including Sales Leaders. Within three business days, the firms had responded with specific questions about MarCom's situation along with some general thoughts and recommendations. By Thursday afternoon, John had collected the necessary information about the three firms and started composing a recommendation to present to Stephen and Mary. He planned to finish it by Tuesday and make final refinements to his recommendations just prior to his presentation on Wednesday. John's wife was not going to like it, but he would have to spend the weekend putting his findings and recommendations on paper.

By Monday morning, John had completed his recommendations for the sales process initiative. He called Stephen's administrative assistant, Julie, to schedule some time with Stephen and Mary on Wednesday afternoon to present his findings. The meeting was set for 2:00 P.M. After scheduling the meeting, John headed down the hall to the conference room for the weekly Monday morning sales meeting.

"Good morning, guys!" John exclaimed to the sales team.

"Hi, John. How was your weekend?" Robert Hunte, a senior salesperson, piped up.

"It was great, Robert. Thanks for asking. Okay, let's dive into this week's sales reports. Robert, let's start with you."

Robert sat forward in his chair. "I've been working on a couple of big opportunities over the past several weeks; one of which, I hope to have an answer on by the end of this week."

"Who's the account with?" John asked.

"The company is Best in the West Restaurants. They're a new franchise operator with 20 family steakhouse restaurants," Robert replied.

"How did you hear about them?" John probed.

"A friend of mine introduced me to the VP of Marketing several months ago. After a number of conversations with him, I learned that Best in the West wasn't doing much direct marketing. So, I sent their VP of Marketing a proposal suggesting that they try direct mailing in areas surrounding their restaurants to stimulate more retail traffic."

"What's the name of the VP of Marketing?" asked John.

"Bob West," Robert replied. "I think that this could be a half million dollar account, John."

"How do you figure that?" asked John quizzed him.

"Well, I figure that Bob probably spent in excess of a half a million dollars last year on radio advertising alone. We could easily divert some of those dollars to direct marketing and demonstrate a measurable ROI."

"I like your thinking," started John. "I'd like to talk with you further about this opportunity and see if we have some Internet marketing opportunities with this account. What else do you have going?"

"I've been working on some accounts in the residential real estate market."

"Tell us more," John replied.

"Well, I've been having conversations with some seasoned real estate agents, and they're telling me that their agencies are trying everything under the sun to get interested parties to either sell their current home or buy a new one. I'm not sure what the best approach would be, but I think that we could be helpful in creating effective d/m tactics."

"Robert, I'm not sure where you're heading with this one, but maybe this is an opportunity for you and me to put our heads together and see if there's anything there. Do you have anything else to report?"

"No. That's it for now, John."

The rest of the representatives gave their reports just as Robert had. The results of the sales meeting left John feeling anxious. As far as he could tell, the sales pipeline was not looking healthy. None of his representatives foresaw major opportunities on the horizon. Furthermore, over the last few years the business had generated an average CAGR of 3 percent and the economy was getting tighter.

Mary was at her desk, reviewing John's latest sales forecast. As she revisited the previous month's reports, she became increasingly frustrated. She knew that MarCom's sales forecasts had never been very accurate, which she had tried to compensate for by employing an algorithm that included a sliding scale that predicted the sales forecast for the next 30, 60, and 90 days. Amazingly, her estimates almost matched actual sales revenues, her predictions allowing for a difference of ±3 percentage points for the 30-day forecast, ±5 percentage points in the 60-day forecast and ±7 percentage points in the 90-day forecast. Although it was not an ideal approach for forecasting revenues, it was preferable to the sales teams' inaccurate data. Mary hoped that John's recommendations at their upcoming meeting would signal a new sales philosophy that dramatically improved MarCom's sales forecasting accuracy, which would lead to other sales process improvements.

At 2:00 P.M. on Wednesday afternoon, John was already in the conference room reviewing his findings and recommendations. He had decided to present them from hard copy instead of attempting to deliver a PowerPoint presentation.

Stephen and Mary walked into the conference room and greeted John with a smile.

"Hi Stephen and Mary. How are you this afternoon?"

"Great," Stephen said. "I'm eager to hear what you've come up with."

"Well, I've been doing some research, and I've come up with an approach that I believe is the best path to get us to where we want to go."

"Great, John," Stephen replied. "Let's see what you've got."

John passed around a three-page document. The first page spoke to the situation that MarCom was currently facing concerning its selling process and the lack of accuracy in sales forecasting. John outlined three critical issues faced by MarCom's sales team.

CRITICAL ISSUES
- Lack of a repeatable, consistently deployable selling process
- Lack of sales forecasting accuracy
- Lack of quality new business opportunities offered up by the sales team

John then outlined some primary objectives for addressing the sales teams' shortcomings.

OBJECTIVES
- Define, implement, and adhere to a proven, quality sales process.
- Generate a minimum of 7 percent sales growth in the first 12 months following the implementation of the new sales process.

Page two of John's recommendation detailed a strategy to accomplish the stated objectives.

RECOMMENDED STRATEGIES

Process: Engage a sales management consulting firm experienced in engineering and implementing proven sales processes with small to mid-tier clients.

People: Assess the current sales people to provide a benchmark for the organization and begin to "top-grade" the sales force.

Following the recommended strategies, John outlined a budget with a timeline for Stephen and Mary, basing it on the research he had done with the three prospective firms.

BUDGET

Phase 1: Discovery and Recommendations ($15K-$25K)

Phase 2: Process Implementation ($30K-$50K)

Phase 3: Sales Training for Process Adherence ($3K per rep.)

TIMING

Phase 1: Discovery and Recommendations (15-20 days from start)

Phase 2: Process Implementation (30-45 days from start)

Phase 3: Sales Training for Process Adherence (30-45 days from process implementation with follow-up training once a month for six months)

Once John had presented his plan, Stephen offered a few comments and questions.

"John, I think you're heading in the right direction. You've hit our critical issues on the head. Do you have any idea as to what firm we should go with?"

"I've been speaking with three firms and I'd like to speak with their references. Before I do that, though, I want to develop a simple questionnaire where I ask the same questions of each potential firm. In the end, I'd like bring in the top two firms for interviews."

"Good thinking, John," Stephen replied

Stephen turned to Mary. "Do you have any questions or comments?"

"I have a couple of thoughts," Mary began. "I agree that you've hit the nail on the head with respect to the critical issues and your statement of objectives, but, at risk of sounding like a broken record, one area that continues to concern me is sales forecasting accuracy. Where do you see this issue being addressed?"

John paused for a moment. "Based on my conversations with the consultants, I've been assured that, once we define and implement a new sales process, we'll begin to see improved sales forecasting. So, we need to discuss these predictions with the prospective sales and marketing consultants and find out how they've addressed accuracy in sales forecasting."

Key Takeaways From Chapter 2

The problems facing the MarCom agency unfortunately are common. The failure to define business processes such that the organization simply is running rudderless with no clear direction is not only inefficient but creates additional hurdles in achieving the organization's goals and objectives. The following summarizes the key weaknesses that exist within the MarCom agency.

LACK OF LEADERSHIP
- Failure to form a vision for the agency
- Failure to set expectations with management to establish operating procedures for all company units

LACK OF PROCESS
- No tested and proven sales process
- No process for project management
- No process for account growth and development

LACK OF APPROACH FOR MARKETING MARCOM
- No strategy in place for positioning the agency
- No advertising and/or promotion of the agency
- Failure to effectively leverage the agency's web presence
  - —No keyword research
  - —No optimization of the site for SEO
  - —No use of the agency's site to capture data on visitors
  - —No email marketing to either prospects or clients

MarCom's management had modestly grown the agency's business despite several managerial and operational weaknesses. Going forward, these issues would have to be addressed as competition grows keener and more sophisticated buyers enter the market. Failure to get its own house in order would seriously compromise MarCom's ability to be a viable agency in the long term.

Mary agreed. Then Stephen turned to John. "What are our next steps?"

"Well, we haven't talked about budget. What's your reaction to the numbers?" John replied.

"I think we need to see some formal proposals from the consulting firms, but I think that the budget ranges you've outlined are reasonable. This is a serious issue for us, and if we do this right, we'll be in a much stronger position to grow the business than we are in today. So, what are our next steps?"

"I'd like to spend the next couple of days putting together the questionnaire that I'll be using to interview prospective consulting firms," John replied. "Then I'll run it by you and Mary to make sure that I've captured the key points that we need to address. How's that for a first step?"

"I like it John," Stephen smiled. "How about having your draft on my desk by the close of business on Friday?"

"No problem. Is there anything else that we should address?"

"I don't think so," yawned Stephen. "You've done a good job here. I look forward to seeing this project underway and the benefits that the agency will reap once it is."

With that, Stephen, Mary and John left the conference room, feeling as if they had made real progress. MarCom was a well-established marketing services agency, but much of its failure to grow beyond a small agency was due its failure to reinvent and continuously improve both the services that it delivered to its clients and the manner in which it delivered them. MarCom's problems had started at the top and had trickled down.

3
The World According to GroupOne

When it was founded in September 2005, GroupOne's company values were inspired by the Hurricane Katrina disaster that struck the US Gulf Coast. As the storm descended, GroupOne's founder, Paul Austin, was contemplating the agency's charter and mission statement when they suddenly became clear. Instead of becoming a marketing services agency that only helped companies whose sales and marketing teams were weathering the "storms" of ineffective sales and marketing techniques, GroupOne would be a community- minded agency committed to making a difference in the larger community—an approach that created a values structure that was sorely missing in the marketing services industry.

In the agency's early days, Paul and several of his new hires made a pilgrimage to New Orleans and camped out in disaster shelters to assist the Red Cross. When they returned home, they decided to devise a way to offer the Gulf Coast region their continuing support. In its first year of operation, GroupOne contributed 10 percent of its net operating income to the Katrina relief effort. Although it was not much, their first gift of $5,000, when combined with similar efforts by other small companies, went a long way toward helping the residents of New Orleans put their lives back together. Over the next three years, GroupOne contributed over $50,000 to rebuilding New Orleans and the lives of its residents, making good on its commitment to support the clean-up effort until the job was finished.

GroupOne's response to Hurricane Katrina lends valuable insight into the kind of values-based business that Paul had in mind when he formed the agency. GroupOne was a for-profit marketing services agency, but it was more than that to its shareholders and stakeholders; it was a business with a conscience—a company that consistently achieved its humanitarian and financial goals.

Paul was a young man who had spent his 15-year career in marketing. The first 8 years of his career were spent working for a major consumer package goods (CPG) marketer. He began as a brand manager and eventually became VP and Director of Marketing for a segment of the company's premium brands. Although successful, he felt hampered by the stolid atmosphere of the corporate environment. Consequently, after eight years of working for a multinational Fortune 500 corporation, he went to work as an account manager for a mid-size ad agency and, four years later, decided to form his own agency.

Before he formed GroupOne, Paul knew what kind of culture he wanted for his company. In addition to GroupOne's caring for something larger than itself, Paul wanted every employee to feel a sense of ownership in the business. Working with his lawyer and his accountant, he set up an employee stock ownership plan (ESOP) that gave employees the opportunity to purchase stock. Managerial employees would receive voting shares, while others were granted nonvoting stock.

To manage GroupOne's day-to-day operations, Paul hired Susan Chapman, the Director of Account Services for the ad agency he had previously worked at. Her attention to detail and her people skills were superb. She had a reputation for being a sound strategic thinker coupled with a great sense of what tactical requirements were necessary to complete jobs on time and on budget. Paul felt fortunate to have attracted Susan to GroupOne, but it was not hard to build a team of great people when the team captain was such an outstanding person.

Paul's next hire was GroupOne's controller. He was looking for someone with agency experience and requisite accounting credentials. After a month of searching, he found Jonathan Steward. After thoroughly reviewing his credentials, work experience, and references, Paul contacted Jonathan for an interview. The first interview went well, and Paul invited Jonathan to interview with GroupOne's other executives. Within three weeks, the interviews were completed, and Paul extended Jonathan an offer that was quickly accepted.

Next, Paul began looking for a senior sales executive with 5 to 10 years of agency experience in new business development. Realizing that connecting with a client's senior management at a strategic level would make the relationship more beneficial to both parties, Paul was interested in attracting clients that were looking for a strategic partner in their agency. Therefore, the sales executive needed to possess a high degree of strategic marketing expertise. He or she also needed to be process oriented, working effectively with clients through the customer buying process, and, by extension, working effectively with other members of GroupOne.

After doing some in-depth networking through management recruiters, Paul found his sales executive in Brian Walker. Brian had been in the advertising agency business for 17 years. His easy-going optimism and affable sense of humor made a great first impression, and his success in business development was legendary. In his last position as SVP of business development for a mid-size agency in Milwaukee, he and his team of five account executives doubled the agency's gross billings from $50 to $100 million in only five years. Half of the growth came from expanded relationships with existing accounts and the other half came from new account/client acquisition. Brian learned early on that a sophisticated demand generation program with multitouch, multichannel communications combining the effective use of online and offline communications had the potential to play a valuable role in developing prospect and client relationships. In other words, when a business executive is considering hiring a new agency, the first agency that usually comes to mind is the agency with which he or she has had a longstanding dialogue.

To help accomplish GroupOne's growth plans, Paul decided to hire a senior marketing strategist to support both the marketing of the agency's services and its client assignments at a strategic level. He was looking for a seasoned marketing professional with 7 to 12 years of both client-side and agency experience. After months of consulting with management recruiters and his own network, Paul found the perfect person for the job in Stephanie Atwood. For the past seven years, Stephanie had worked as director of marketing for new products at a computer-manufacturing firm in Silicon Valley. Before her current position, she spent five years as head of strategic planning for a large ad agency in the San Francisco Bay area. She received her MBA from Stanford and her undergraduate degree in finance from UCLA.

Although Stephanie enjoyed her work in the high-tech industry, she was anxious to get back into the agency world for the many client marketing and communications challenges that it offered. One Friday afternoon, as she was packing her briefcase with take-home work, Stephanie received a call from a management recruiter who was representing a client in the ad agency business. The agent explained that the company had been in business for three years, but had already displayed great performance in landing a number of impressive clients. The more Stephanie heard, the more interested she became in GroupOne. Her first phone conversation with Paul was one that she would never forget. Paul explained GroupOne's company vision and spoke of how their common client-side experiences—his with a CPG firm and hers in the computer-manufacturing field—placed them on common ground. After asking several questions of Paul, Stephanie accepted his invitation to come to the agency for a more in-depth conversation.

Two weeks later, Stephanie was on a plane to visit with Paul and the members of his senior management team. She was a bit nervous, but her anxiety was eased when she met Paul. Stephanie found Paul to be a breath of fresh air. His vision for the agency and the types of clients they had already attracted were incredible. Stephanie met individually with the other members of the executive team. She and Brian hit it off immediately, sharing a similar view of how the disciplines of sales and marketing should work together to grow business in a cost effective manner.

After meeting with Brian, Stephanie met Susan. They quickly found themselves on the same page concerning client services and the valuable role played by the account services team from both a strategic and tactical program execution perspective. Stephanie was feeling good about the team that Paul had assembled. The only person that she had yet to meet was the GroupOne's controller.

Stephanie's meeting with Jonathan Steward went as well as her meetings with the other members of GroupOne's management. Jonathan had 10 years of experience as a company controller in a large agency before he joined GroupOne. He was formally educated as an accountant and went on to become a licensed CPA. His expansive knowledge of agency accounting practices was impressive. He and Stephanie spoke at length about assessing client profitability and the direction that

GroupOne was taking to strengthen the profitability and long-term value of its client relationships.

Before Paul extended Stephanie an offer, he conferred with his management team, which gave Stephanie unanimous approval. There was nothing left to do but to extend her an offer. Within a week after her interviews, Paul extended Stephanie a formal offer that she immediately accepted. She was officially GroupOne's VP of Marketing and Strategy Development. Paul felt fortunate to have assembled such a great leadership team.

Brian Walker had been with GroupOne since early 2006. In those days, most of Brian's work centered on securing new business for the agency. However, as the agency began to acquire new accounts, he necessarily began searching for experienced, proven sales people who were like "hunters" in the way that they pursued new business opportunities, but were equally able to grow client business by "farming" the relationships, which means taking the time to understand client business issues and then developing well conceived marketing solutions to address the issues.

Brian's first hire was Molly McBride—a bright, experienced sales professional. Molly had worked with other local agencies, but she had not found an agency with the right culture. Performance was never an issue for Molly. Her ability to understand client issues and work closely with them to design solutions that yielded measurable results with consistently positive returns on her client's investments meant that she consistently exceeded her sales quotas.

The next account executive hired by GroupOne was Wallace Jones. His production ranked second to Molly's, but he was a sound strategic thinker and a consistent performer. Paul wanted his sales team to be racially and culturally diverse, making Wallace—an African-American—a positive cultural move for the agency. Before joining GroupOne, Wallace had worked with another database marketing services firm where his work focused on the high-tech vertical.

The third account executive who Brian hired was Jason Austin. Jason came to the agency from the client side of the business. A seven-year brand manager for a Fortune 100 multinational company, Jason, like many successful young managers working for large corporations, was interested in finding a smaller company with a culture that was more to his liking. Jason had been with GroupOne for two years and had done well. Clients appreciated his business/marketing knowledge and expertise, and although he was not the top sales producer, he consistently met his sales quota.

The fourth account executive was Megan Phillips. Megan, like the other account executives, was a solid performer. Having previously worked for a larger traditional ad agency, the discipline of database marketing was new to her, but she quickly learned the ropes and put together some impressive programs that exceeded her clients' expectations regarding business development and return on investment.

The fifth and final account executive was Steve Basler. Steve, like Jason, came from the client side of the business. He was a brand director for a small regional telecommunications/cable services operator. He became acquainted with GroupOne through work that GroupOne had done for one of his company's business units in

Exhibit 3-1. Alignment of Customer Buying with Enterprise Selling Process

the western states. Steve was impressed with Paul, Brian, and their idea of working with his company to identify its business/marketing issues and then addressing the issues with integrated marketing tactics. Since joining GroupOne a year and a half ago, Steve had consistently met his quarterly and annual sales targets. Given his work experience, Brian requested that Steve focus his efforts on the telecommunications services sector. The strategy proved to be a sound one: Steve successfully attracted a number of regional telecom clients, as well as larger national service providers that had smaller projects that fit the capacity of the agency.

The secret to GroupOne's sales success was actually no secret. From the start, Brian focused on putting in place a selling process that mirrored the customer/client's buying process. The focus was not on what GroupOne was interested in selling, but on the needs of the customer and what the customer was prepared to buy. By employing a customer-oriented selling process, GroupOne consistently won more client engagements than its competitors. To help the account executives and account services personnel understand the details behind the customer buying and enterprise selling processes, Brian worked with a sales and marketing consulting firm to detail the two processes and express them in a simple format.

Brian found the diagram (Exhibit 3-1) of the independent yet interconnected processes helpful on three fronts: It gave team members a clear understanding of the process that each of them would follow in acquiring new business; it allowed him to follow each salesperson's sales process to determine a customer's position in the buying process; and he was able to chart where his account executives were at in the selling process. From a sales management perspective, ensuring that his sales people were adhering to the process was critically important to sales effectiveness. Understanding where prospective customers were at in the process gave Brian better insight into the sales pipeline and the probability of closure for each of the opportunities therein, resulting in a high degree of sales forecasting accuracy. From a selling perspective, the diagram placed account executives in a better position to assess their own progress and determine what phase of the process they were in with a prospective client. In the final analysis, the definition and documentation of the selling process provided a proven and repeatable approach to generating new business for GroupOne.

The role of Stephanie Atwood and her marketing team was rather simple: They had to help the sales team *sell*. However, they had to do more than just generate qualified leads for the account executives. Stephanie and Brian came up with an integrated marketing communications process that created an ongoing dialogue with current and prospective clients to identify specific goals that their companies wanted to achieve.

The first step in getting the sales and marketing team on the same page was to define what constituted a "qualified lead." The definition became clear by defining the client specific goals that GroupOne would be in a position to address. Stephanie and her team then put together a multitouch, integrated demand generation plan with all of the requisite communications elements, from outbound call scripts for the telemarketing team, to direct mail pieces, email campaigns, and SEO strategies for the web site. The demand generation program had been in place for more then two years and had proven highly profitable. Within the first two years, the agency realized over a 500 percent ROI on the program.

Since putting the demand generation system in place, GroupOne had added 20 new clients to its roster. At the top end of the roster were 6 publicly traded Fortune 1000 companies that focused on telecommunications, satellite, and cable operations, but the majority of the clients on GroupOne's roster were small to mid-size B2B or B2C businesses that marketed products and/or services, of which Software Solutions, Inc., was a typical example. Like many new wave software development companies, Software Solutions operated as an SaaS solutions provider. The beauty of these solutions was that their applications were available to anyone, anywhere. SaaS providers housed their applications on servers, where any subscriber could access the application via a web browser. Software Solutions provided applications for businesses and individual users that targeted niche markets. For example, two years ago, the company had done extensive research on veterinarians who specialized in treating small animals. From their research, Software Solutions learned that there was no true leader in comprehensive practice management applications. There were a number of players, but none of them offered a comprehensive set of applications that addressed both back office and front office (e.g., POS) applications. Furthermore, almost every application was server-based, requiring extensive database design along with expensive annual maintenance agreements.

Following some extensive quantitative research to assess market demand, interest, and revenue potential, Software Solutions began a major development effort to create a comprehensive SaaS solution for small-animal practitioners. They called the application PracticeOne. After much discussion and negotiation, the company received the Small Animal Hospital Association's coveted seal of approval for PracticeOne. The program appealed to small animal practitioners by offering marketing applications and comprehensive solutions to everything from patient case management to accounting and vendor management. The practice owner did not have to invest in additional hardware to operate the application or pay for expensive annual software upgrades. The contracting veterinary hospital simply paid a low monthly fee on a one-year renewable contract. PracticeOne improved the quality of practice administration, patient care and, at the same time, reduced operating expenses.

Bryce McLaughlin was the founder and chief technology innovator of Software Solutions. One of his associates recommended GroupOne to help with Software Solutions' launch and marketing of PracticeOne. After several meetings with GroupOne and other agencies, Bryce decided on GroupOne. At their first meeting, Paul brought his best resources to the table, asking Stephanie, Brian and members of their respective support teams to join him in the meeting. After everyone was introduced, Paul went on to say how GroupOne was committed to the successful launch of PracticeOne. Following his introductory comments, Paul turned to Bryce and asked if he had anything to share with the group.

"Paul," Bryce began, "thank you for bringing your associates to this meeting. I also applaud you for the organization you've been able to build at GroupOne. Though we haven't been down in the trenches together yet, I feel like I have a good idea of what your agency is about. I spent considerable time speaking with your current and past clients, and I don't think I've ever heard an agency praised so highly. Your record of success with your clients is remarkable, and it's apparent that you and I share the belief that it's not enough to just have a great idea, product, or service. You need quality people executing an intelligent plan. Otherwise, products and services—and their companies—never realize their full potential.

"Thanks for the kind words, Bryce. Stephanie, do you want to kick things off and lead our discussion."

"Thanks, Paul. Let's get started." Stephanie stood up and made her way to the whiteboard.

PracticeOne, like so many other product launches and integrated marketing campaigns that GroupOne had previously designed and executed, exceeded it's first six-month revenue forecast and market penetration rate. GroupOne had put in place a fully integrated marketing plan that consisted of direct mail, email, web presence, and trade show and PR initiatives. As with other programs designed by the agency, key metrics that measured success and then measured and tracked the performance of customer acquisition by each of the communications channels came first. GroupOne implemented split cell tests to assess the effectiveness of various tactics and to measure the ROI within each of the combinations of tactics deployed. Concerning direct marketing efforts, GroupOne brainstormed with Software Solutions to put together a list of source strategies that captured a comprehensive list of small animal practitioners within targeted geographic markets.

After the first full year in the market, PracticeOne had far exceeded the revenues and market penetration set forth in the original plan. Bryce McLaughlin could not say enough about the performance of the programs designed and executed by GroupOne. After the first 12 months on the market, PracticeOne had racked-up the following impressive statistics.

CUSTOMER ACQUISITION & MARKET PENETRATION
- Achieved a 12 percent penetration of small animal practices vs. a goal of 7 percent.

REVENUE & PROFITS
- Exceeded revenue targets for the business by 25 percent.
- Exceeded net operating income targets by 30 percent.

RETURN ON MARKETING INVESTMENT
- Achieved a return on marketing investment (ROMI) of 145 percent.

CUSTOMER SATISFACTION
- Achieved a customer satisfaction score of 6.5 on a scale of 1 to 7.
- Realized a Customer Referral Rate (CRR) of 20 percent (i.e., of the customers signed up for the service, 20 percent recommended the service to one or more other small animal practitioners).

CUSTOMER RETENTION
- By the end of month 12, retained 95 percent of customers that originally signed up.

Although the statistics were impressive, they did not represent GroupOne's usual performance metrics. GroupOne knew how to produce large numbers, but it was equally concerned with measuring such numbers in a realistic way. As they had done for Software Solutions, they initially took time to define the measures of success. Part of this process was based on GroupOne's appreciation of a famous quote arguably attributed to either Peter Drucker or Lord Kelvin: "What gets measured, gets done."

Success for GroupOne and its clients was not hard to understand, for it was predicated on three simple elements:

PEOPLE
When Paul Austin founded GroupOne, he knew that the only way to be successful was to surround himself with bright, hard working people that consistently displayed a "can-do" attitude. He was fortunate to find such people early on. Every member of his management team exemplified the qualities that he had hoped to bring to the organization. An outstanding team had created an outstanding agency.

PROCESS
At heart of the GroupOne's consistent performance was its dedication to defining, refining and adhering to quality process, whether in account service,

Key Takeaways from Chapter 3

GroupOne's success was a result of quality leadership and assembling a management team with expert skills and experience. Jim Collins, author of *Built to Last* and *Good to Great* learned in his analysis of businesses that one of the most important predictors of high-level success is having the right people on board. Collins learned that, once an organization gets the "right people on the bus" and then makes certain to get the "right people" in the "right seats," a critical element of driving business success is in place.

GroupOne knew from the outset that, in order to more than an average marketing services agency, it would be necessary to search for the right people to handle key management functions. Being a well-funded start-up, GroupOne started off on the right foot: It was instantly in a position to extend attractive, highly competitive salary offers to quality talent. To round out its executive compensation plan, GroupOne's key managers were offered the opportunity to either earn or purchase an equity position in the firm. That sense of ownership and the potential to build individual net worth as a result of the fruits of the team's labor added to the value of being a member of GroupOne, thus enhancing GroupOne's prospects of retaining its top talent over the long term.

Although having well-defined business processes are critical to effectively managing a business and delivering increasingly better performance, it is equally important to build the organization on the shoulders of an expert management team that possesses sound character, integrity and a desire to serve customers and fellow employees alike.

---

finance and accounting, or sales and marketing. The extra time and effort that the agency took to define the selling process and the customer buying process provided a solid foundation for understanding and effectively managing the sales and marketing process.

COMMITMENT TO SERVE

Following Paul's original vision for GroupOne, the management team embraced the philosophy that its work would be defined by community interest. By focusing on hiring the "right" people, employing the "right" processes and embracing a commitment to serving its clients and the community, GroupOne had become an outstanding service provider.

4
Advanced Technologies Meets MarCom Solutions

The day following his strategic planning session with AT, Joe Albright began working to insure that the action items were completed by the dates that he and the Scotts had agreed to at the close of their session.

The first item on his To Do list was searching for a marketing services agency. However, before reaching out to a prospective agency partner, Joe needed to detail the marketing requirements for SecureSoft. To insure that the agencies he would be contacting were all on the same page, he would put together a formal Request for Proposal (RFP) that outlined AT's current situation regarding SecureSoft. The RFP would also outline the desired results from a B2B demand generation program. However, in order to get a good idea of how the agencies responding to the RFP would approach the process, Joe avoided laying down a detailed map of AT's marketing plan.

As a follow-up to AT's two-day planning session, Joe called Frank early Wednesday morning to see how he was progressing with the search for the sales executive.

"Good morning, Frank. It's Joe. I thought I'd check in with you to see how the search for a sales executive is coming along."

"Joe, there's no moss growing under your feet. I just got off of the phone with a recruiter friend of mine. I outlined the position requirements for him, and right now I'm preparing an email detailing those requirements. I'll be forwarding it to the recruiter, and I'll copy you and Marlie on the document before sending it."

"Great, Frank. I'll look forward to seeing it." Joe went on to give Frank an update on his activities. "I've started putting together an RFP that will go out to three or four agencies that I believe have the potential to do a great job for your company. I plan on getting that out no later than tomorrow morning. The agencies will have 10 working days to respond. That way, we can still entertain their presentations for 30 days."

"Okay, Joe. Thanks for the call and all of your support over the past two days. I think we had a productive session."

"No problem, Frank. I think we've got a good start as well. Call me if anything comes up. Take care."

Joe spent the next two hours putting the finishing touches on the RFP. With the RFP ready to go, the next step was to identify possible agency partners. Joe consulted his database of suppliers and agencies that had been recommended to him in the past, coming up with four agencies that seemed to fit AT's needs. The first agency that Joe selected, The Foster Agency, was almost exclusively a B2B agency. Founded by long-time ad man, David Foster, the agency had been in business for almost eight years. Since its inception, The Foster Agency had grown to approximately 45 employees and approximately $18 million in gross revenues.

The next agency, MarCom Solutions, had been in business for more than 20 years. Joe had heard good things about MarCom, but the current word on the street was that they were long on tactics and short on strategy. Nonetheless, Joe felt that AT had nothing to lose by forwarding them an RFP to see what kind of response they would put together.

The third agency on the list, Slone Direct, was primarily a direct marketing/mail agency, focusing on B2B client work. Slone had been in business for nearly ten years with a client list of mostly mid-size companies.

The final agency, GroupOne, was the youngest of the agencies, having opened in late 2005. However, Joe had heard some impressive reports of their work. Unlike MarCom, GroupOne was long on strategy, but strong on tactical implementation as well. Understanding that failure to execute integrated multitouch, cross-channel campaigns risks delivering less than optimum program performance, they prided themselves on the quality of their tactical campaigns.

Joe contacted each of the four agencies to obtain contact information for one of their account executives or senior sales people to whom he would present the RFP. Each of the representatives at the four agencies was receptive to receiving the RFP and agreed to respond within 10 business days. Joe informed each representative that, in 4 days, he would hold a conference call where all four agencies could present any questions regarding the RFP.

After completing the phone calls, Joe composed an email that contained all of the necessary conference call details, blind copied Frank and Marlie on the message, attached the RFP, and forwarded the message to the four agencies. Then he began working on the remaining list of tasks that came out of the strategic planning session.

The next item on Joe's list was the preparation of a sales plan. The task list prepared at the strategic planning session called for the plan to be completed within 10 days of the close of the planning session, giving Joe plenty of time to complete it. He was anxious to explore the plan's development on two fronts. First, he considered that the sales plan, even in its early stages, could provide a great starting point for the new sales executive that AT would be hiring within the next two months. Second, he felt that the plan could provide a road map for the demand generation program that would be coming from the hired agency.

Joe started developing his outline for the sales plan. His first step was to envision SecureSoft's ideal customers. The traditional approach to this matter would be to analyze the current customer base by profiling it and then segmenting the larger profile into smaller, more targeted segments. However, because SecureSoft was a new product, there was no product history or customer data from which to draw insight. Thus, in lieu of having customer data to analyze, the logical approach was to review primary quantitative research in order to uncover pockets of interest by industry vertical, company size, or a similar demo/firmographic data.

Unfortunately, AT had not invested in primary research prior to SecureSoft's launch. But instead of taking wild guesses at defining SecureSoft's target market, Joe decided to analyze the target market of a competitive product whose attributes were similar to SecureSoft's. Yet, once again, he hit a roadblock, for SecureSoft really had no direct competitors. All that Joe could do was go with his experience, which led him to believe that SecureSoft's best opportunities existed with businesses whose main concerns revolved around documentation and proprietary data. Upon brainstorming some industry verticals, he arrived at seven industry segments that, at face value, were good candidates for the SecureSoft solution:

- Accounting
- Architects
- Attorneys
- Banking
- Healthcare Services
- Healthcare Insurance
- Investment Services

Joe needed to do some secondary research to determine the size of the opportunities in each vertical. He, Frank, and Marlie had discussed that geography would not be a parameter or constraint for market opportunity. After all, SecureSoft was delivered as a SaaS solution, which made it available to any company anywhere in the world. But they had to start somewhere, and Joe thought it best to begin by identifying the number of American companies that fell within the seven verticals, with international opportunities comprising phase two of the sales plan. He used his list broker resources to come up with list counts by vertical. From there, he could expand or contract the size of the prospect universe based on company size and geographic proximity to AT's headquarters.

John Moloney at MarCom Solutions received Joe's call regarding AT's RFP and quickly retrieved the email that detailed the timing and events relating to the RFP response. After reviewing the RFP, John called a meeting with one of his sales reps and Christine Marquette to assemble a team that would address the RFP. At this point, John was unclear on the scope of MarCom's opportunity with AT and he did not want to involve significant agency resources until he secured more information.

John sent out a meeting invite to Christine and senior salesperson, Robert Hunte. Robert had a track record of dealing with technology businesses, and John felt that Robert's experience might come in handy. After receiving Robert and Christine's responses to the meeting invite on Wednesday afternoon, John set the meeting for the next morning at 9:00 A.M.

At 9:00 A.M. sharp, John kicked off the meeting with a summary of the telephone conversation that he had had with Joe. He then handled out AT's five-page RFP along with a copy of the email detailing the timeline for the response and the vendor conference call that would take place on Tuesday of the coming week. The RFP response was due by 5:00 P.M. the following Wednesday. John walked through the RFP with Christine and Robert, thoroughly reviewing the facts in the "current situation" section along with the objectives that AT had set forth in its marketing plan. After 15 minutes of reviewing the RFP, John asked for Christine and Robert's opinion.

"John, this is pretty interesting stuff, but I'm not sure these folks know what they want." Robert was never shy about sharing his opinions, which, more often than not, indicated that he felt a client was not terribly smart.

"I'm not following you, Robert. What do you mean?" John replied.

"Well, they've done a good job of providing us with background on the business and an early track record of SecureSoft, of which there isn't much, but they haven't told us what they want us to *do*."

John placed his hand on his forehead, rubbing it like he was fighting off the early stages of a migraine. "Robert, I think that it's up to us to come up with the marketing tactics to achieve the objectives that they've set forth. Christine, what do you think?"

"I'm concerned that we might expend a lot of resources and find that these people don't have the budget to do what needs to be done."

"Fair point," John replied. "Robert, why don't you do a little homework on this company and see what you can learn. You can probably get a D&B on them. I don't want you to spend too much time delving into their financial health, but we should know whether they're in a position to pay the bills when we start doing the work."

"I'll get right on it, John," said Robert.

John wanted to reconvene with Christine and Robert to discuss the details of their response to the RFP. "On Tuesday of next week, we'll be participating in a vendor conference call with the consultant overseeing the RFP process. I'd like for us to spend some time reading and thinking through this RFP to come up with a list of questions that we need answered in order to do a proper job of responding to the RFP. Let's each put some questions on paper over the next 24 hours. After that, I'll compile the list of official questions and get them back to the team. Does that work for both of you?"

"Makes sense, John," Christine replied.

"I'll get you my thoughts to you by noon tomorrow," Robert chimed in. "I have a number of client meetings tomorrow, but I should be able to get you something by the close of business tomorrow," Christine continued.

"Thanks, guys," replied John. "Robert, I'd like for you to draft the response to the RFP. I'm sure that Christine will be able to lend a hand once you've put together a first draft. There's no need to start from scratch on this thing. We've got a number of RFP responses in our resource library that you can lift content from, and you'll probably find a B2B customer acquisition program on the company server that comes close to fitting the bill."

Robert thought for a moment. "No problem, John. I can do that. As a matter of fact, if I remember correctly, I put together a proposal last month for a B2B client that would probably be a perfect solution to this situation."

"Perfect," John said. "Let me know if you need any help along the way. Is there anything else we need to discuss?"

"I don't think so." Christine replied.

"I agree." Robert responded. "I think that this one is pretty straightforward."

"Good enough. I look forward to receiving your questions tomorrow. Have a good day."

"You too, John," Christine and Robert replied.

After Robert and Christine left the conference room, John sat back in his chair to reflect on where MarCom appeared to be heading in its response to AT's RFP. The opportunity had arrived out of the blue from a sales and marketing consultant he had never met, which made him suspect that there were probably two or three other agencies competing for the job. He thought it would be good idea to jot down some post meeting thoughts to ask the AT sales and marketing consultant during the conference call next Tuesday.

QUESTIONS REGARDING SECURESOFT

1. What have been the results of early sales calls for SecureSoft?
2. Has AT used direct marketing programs in support of SecureSoft?
   a. If yes, describe the campaign and its results?
   b. If not, why not?
3. How will AT define success of future marketing efforts?
4. What is AT's sales and marketing budget?
5. What criteria will AT use when comparing agencies?

After jotting down his questions, John returned to his office to catch up on some emails. He thought that it would be wise to send Joe an email to let him know that MarCom would be participating in the conference call and that he was looking forward to receiving the details about the conference call.

At noon on the following day, John found a new message from Christine with the subject line: "Discovery Questions for AT RFP." Upon opening the email, he could see that Christine had put some thought into her responses. For the most part, her questions focused on gathering historical information from AT's previous tactical campaigns. Later that afternoon, John checked his email and found that Robert had yet to submit his questions. He decided to give Robert a call to see where he stood. The phone rang and rang and finally went to voice mail. After leaving Robert a message requesting his questions, John went back to addressing his email messages. After tending to his emails, he turned off his computer and left the office for home.

On Friday morning, John was completing his project on sales process and the recruiting of a sales consulting firm. A week ago, he presented Stephen and Mary with a list of questions he be would asking the prospective firms. To move the process along, he decided to stop by Stephen and Mary's offices to see if they had any input on the questions. Stephen was at his desk.

"Hi, Stephen."

"Hi John. I'm sorry I didn't get back to you about your questions for the consulting firm. It's been another one of those weeks."

"Oh, I understand. Is now an OK time to talk about the questions?" John asked.

"Sure, come on in. Overall, I like your questions, but I have a couple more that I think should be added to the list. First, I'd like to ask the consulting firm how many projects they've undertaken in the past that entailed sales process engineering and re-engineering. Second, I'd also like to know the specifics of each project and the overall results. Along the same lines, I'd ask them to identify their greatest success and their greatest failure and what led to each one."

"No problem. Is there anything else you'd like to add?"

"No, John. I think you've got the bases well covered. What are your next steps?"

"I plan to get input from Mary and then contact the three firms and get these questions in their hands," John replied.

"Great. Do you think we'll be able to keep to the time table that you outlined for us a week ago?" Stephen asked.

"I don't see why not. I'd like to have a consultant on board within the next three weeks and begin the discovery and recommendations phase immediately thereafter. As I outlined in my recommendations, I envision this phase lasting from 15 to 20 days."

After exchanging goodbyes with Stephen, John went down the hall to talk with Mary. She was not at her desk, so John wrote a not requesting her appraisal of his questions and taped it to her computer monitor. Upon returning to his desk, John checked his email to see if Robert had replied with his thoughts for the RFP questions. At the top of his Inbox was a message from Robert. He apologized that he was unable to get the questions to John on time and then presented three questions:

1. What dollar amount had AT budgeted to market SecureSoft?
2. Has AT defined the list of companies or industries that would be targeted for the marketing campaign(s)? If yes, does a prospect database exist?
3. Are there printed marketing materials for SecureSoft? If yes, could these materials be made available?

John shot Robert a reply and asked Joe the questions that he, Christine, and Robert had compiled. He also took the opportunity to reinforce the fact that MarCom was excited about the prospect of working with AT in the marketing of SecureSoft.

On Tuesday morning of the following week, Joe was ready for the conference calls. To maintain confidentiality, he would hold four separate 30-minute conference calls, one time slot for each agency. MarCom's call was set for 10:00 A.M. At exactly 10, John dialed the conference bridge number. Joe was already on the line. John introduced his people to Joe and proceeded with MarCom's questions.

"Joe, did you have the opportunity to read through the questions that I sent you on Friday."

"I did." Joe replied. "Thanks for sending your questions in advance; it gave me the opportunity to give some thought to my responses."

"You bet, Joe. I thought it might help." John responded.

"Before we get started," began Joe, "I wanted to let you know the ground rules for these question-and-answer sessions. Initially, I considered doing a single session that included all of the firms. That way, all of the prospective vendors would have the opportunity to hear each other's questions. But I've since decided to have separate sessions to provide a degree of confidentiality for the agencies. It will be a little more work on my end, but I think that it will make the process fairer to each agency." Joe paused for a moment, then asked: "Does that sit well with you folks?"

"Yes, it does, Joe" John responded. Thanks for the consideration. Do you want me to start with the questions?"

"Sure. Go ahead," Joe replied.

John asked all of MarCom's questions and received answers to each one. However, Joe gave two answers that caused the MarCom team to scratch their heads, the first of which dealt with budget. Joe said that AT's management team wanted to see what kind of budget the agencies would recommend instead of pre-deciding a budget. The second answer that caused them trouble dealt with AT's criteria for selecting an agency. Joe indicated that there would be three criteria for hiring an agency: the comprehensive nature of an agency's response, an agency's demonstrated experience in designing and executing similar programs, and a demonstrated level of understanding critical factors that AT would have to overcome to achieve their marketing objectives. With five minutes left in the call, John asked Joe to elaborate on the agency evaluation criteria, specifically in terms of price.

"Well, John, we're more concerned about value than we are about cost. We know that we have some challenging issues facing us in the marketing of SecureSoft, and what we're looking for is a marketing partner who can demonstrate that their solutions are going to deliver the greatest value to AT. Funding the marketing effort is another matter. However, when we find the right program, we'll find the money."

Joe needed to bring the call to a close. "Is there anything else?" he asked.

"Not at this point," John replied. "If we have any additional questions, we'd like to get back to you, if that's OK."

"You bet, John," Joe replied. "You folks have a good day."

"You too, Joe. Thanks for your time this morning," ended John, the other team members echoing his sentiment. Joe hung up the receiver.

"*That* was interesting," said Robert.

"What do you mean?" asked John.

"I don't know," Robert replied. "I just thought that the comment about 'value' over 'cost' was a bit strange. After all, sooner or later, price comes into play. I may think that a Lexus delivers incredible value in terms of quality of ride, resale, performance, but, ultimately, I just don't have $50,000 in my pocket to purchase one."

"I understand," began John, "but I believe that Joe thinks that, in order for an agency to win the business, they should be able to demonstrate the value that they deliver in their recommendations." MarCom had never provided a financial cost/benefit analysis in the work that they proposed. Typically, they delivered a proposal that provided a list of tactics accompanied by the cost for each tactic. To determine the cost of the work, a client would combine the cost of each tactic to arrive at a total price for work performed. It was akin to asking a contractor for a bid on remodeling a house. A line-item estimate provided the necessary element of detail as to what was included on the bid and, at the end of the estimate, a total amount stated the cost of the project. MarCom had operated with this sales approach since day one.

John turned to Robert. "Let me ask you *this*, Robert: Knowing what you now know about AT's expectations, how should we approach the positioning of our recommendations?"

Robert stood up from the conference table. "We've had pretty good success with the proposals that I've been putting together as of late. I'd suggest going back to my most recent proposal that closely mirrors what AT is wanting to accomplish and tailor that proposal to fit AT's requirements. We have six working days left to prepare our response and I have a couple of other irons in the fire as well. How about I get my draft of a response to you by the end of Friday. That should give you time to review it over the weekend. Does that work for you?"

"Sounds like a plan," replied John. "I'll look forward to seeing your proposal on Friday."

Robert had the MarCom Solutions proposal on John's desk by noon on Friday. John was in meetings most of the day and did not pick up the proposal until the workday was coming to a close. The proposal was more than thirty pages in length including the appendix. John slid the proposal into his brief case to read at home.

On Sunday afternoon, John opened his brief case and pulled out the draft of the AT proposal prepared by Robert. As he read it, he noticed language that had appeared in other proposals from the agency. All in all, the content was good. Robert had detailed the tactics that would take place over the first six months of the program that he referred to not as a "demand generation program," as was requested on AT's RFP, but as a "customer acquisition program." The proposal contained a line item budget and used client testimonials as a value statement. Under the heading, "delivering value," Robert wrote a note to John: "John, I thought about our conversation on Tuesday concerning the 'value' that MarCom delivers to its clients, and I can't think of a better way to express this value than to have our clients communicate the message. Let me know what you think."

As much as John liked the idea of incorporating client testimonials into the proposal to communicate how MarCom had delivered value to previous clients, he felt that a cost benefit analysis would be stronger. But, without information on AT's financials, such as a profit and loss statement, or average revenue per sale and gross profit margin, there was no way that MarCom could compose a meaningful ROI or "cost benefit analysis." However, John decided that, in the interest of time and team spirit, MarCom should go with the current proposal. After all, John thought, this is the basic approach to proposal writing that has been used at MarCom for years.

John was taking the easy way out. In order to demonstrate "value" and a positive ROI, he needed only to pick up the phone and call Joe to get an answer on the average sale price of a SecureSoft implementation and the associated gross profit margin. With this information in hand, MarCom would have been in a position to produce "best," "probable" and "worst" case ROI scenarios along with a breakeven analysis. This analysis would have clearly communicated the financial value that could potentially be derived from working with MarCom. Failure to go down this path represented a missed opportunity to depict the value represented by the agency's recommendations.

Key Takeaways from Chapter 4

MarCom's business practices are a great example of navigating the sales process using "old school" mindset. In today's highly competitive business environment, customers are constantly looking for answers that demonstrate the tangible value delivered by the seller's product or service offering and providing a prospective customer with a qualitative statement of value (e.g., customer testimonials, references, number of years in business, etc.) alone will not offer sufficient proof of value for a product or service offering. Return on investment (ROI) and return on marketing investment (ROMI) provide tangible evidence of the value expected from a proposed business solution. ROI is a straightforward mathematical calculation. The chart below illustrates the calculations that are used to derive the ROI on an incremental marketing investment. Painting such a financial picture for a business decision-maker provides substantive data upon which intelligent business decisions can be made.

Exhibit 4-1. ROI Breakeven Analysis

	Best	Probable	Worst	Breakeven
Target Population	1,500	1,500	1,500	1,500
Response Rate	1.75%	1.50%	1.25%	0.75%
Conversion Rate	50.00%	45.00%	40.00%	30.00%
New Customers Acquired				
New Customers	13	10	8	3
Unit Volume				
Avg. Number of Units Sold per Customer	1	1	1	1
Average Revenue per Unit Sale	$ 45,000	$ 45,000	$ 45,000	$ 45,000
Revenues				
Revenues from Incremental Marketing Initiatives	$ 585,000	$ 450,000	$ 360,000	$ 135,000
Gross Profit Margin	65.0%	65.0%	65.0%	65.0%
Total Gross Profit	380,000	293,000	234,000	87,750
Marketing Expense				
Integrated Marketing Tactics	$ 87,750	$ 87,750	$ 87,750	$ 87,750
Total Marketing Investment	$ 87,750	$ 87,750	$ 87,750	$ 87,750
EBIT (Earnings before Interest & Tax)	292,250	205,250	146,250	-
Net Profit Margin	50.0%	45.6%	40.6%	0.0%
Discount Rate	1.00	1.00	1.00	1.00
Net Present Value (NPV)	$ 292,250	$ 205,250	$ 146,250	$ -
Individual Customer Value for Pilot - Year 1	$ 22,480	$ 20,530	$ 18,280	$ -
ROI for marketing investment	333%	234%	167%	0%

Note: The calculation of "discount rate" in this model is done so for illustrative purposes. Frequently, when financial projections are estimated over multiple forward years there is a factor incorporated to account for the future value of earnings based on the time value of money to arrive at a calculation of Net Present Value (NPV). The calculations in this model depicts earnings for the present year and thus inserts the factor of "1.0" for the discount rate.

5
Enter GroupOne

When Brian Walker entered his office on Wednesday morning, his desk phone was ringing. He looked at the LED screen on the phone and saw an outside call being forwarded to him by Cynthia, GroupOne's receptionist.

"Brian, it's a call for you from a Joe Albright. Can you take the call?"

"Sure, put him through, Cynthia . . . Mr. Albright?"

"Hey, Brian. How are you?

"Well, I'm not exactly bright eyed and bushy tailed, but how can I help you?"

"I'm a sales and marketing consultant that has been retained by Advanced Technologies to help them in a search for a marketing firm to grow their business. Do you have a few minutes?"

"I certainly do, Joe, please go ahead."

"I'd like to know if GroupOne would be interested in participating in an RFP process. We've identified four prospective agencies as possible partners and our hope is to have all four agencies respond within 10 business days to an RFP that we've prepared. The founders of Advanced Technologies and I will review the responses, which will take 7 working days. Then, based on the responses, we'll decide which of the four agencies to invite in for a formal presentation of recommendations and a brief overview of their agency's experience and capabilities. Is this something that you'd be interested in exploring?"

"Certainly," Brain replied. "When will you be forwarding the RFP?"

"I'll have the RFP out this afternoon. I've also planned for a 30-minute conference call with you and other members of your team to address any questions that you have about the RFP. That call will be scheduled for next Tuesday morning, and I'll include the RFP and conference call details in an email that I'll be sending you later today. Is there anything else that I can answer for you at this time?"

"No, Joe. Your time line is fine. It should be no problem for us to respond to the RFP within ten days. Thanks for considering GroupOne. I look forward receiving your RFP. Do you have my email address?"

"No, I don't. Go ahead and give it to me."

"Joe, before you go, Does Advanced Technologies have a web site?"

"Yes, they do. But, I have to tell you, it's in need of a serious overhaul. That said, if you want to visit their site, the address is advancedtech.biz. Anything else, Brian?"

"No, I think that will do it for now. Thanks again for thinking of GroupOne. We look forward to our next conversation on Tuesday. We'll prepare some questions for you prior to the call."

"Sounds good, Brian." As they wrapped up the call, Joe told Brian to expect the RFP in his inbox after the lunch hour.

As soon as he ended the call, Brian picked up the phone and called Wallace Jones, his number-two account executive. Wallace had several years of experience working with clients in the high-tech verticals. Many of the clients that Wallace had worked with were marketing software solutions with a fast-growing business model that served up hosted software applications, known as SaaS (software as a service) offerings.

"Hi, Wallace. It's Brian. Do you have a few minutes? I have a new business opportunity to discuss with you."

"Sure, Brian. I'll be right over."

Brian sat down with Wallace and outlined the discussion that he had just had with Joe Albright. Along with the summary of the business opportunity, Brian discussed the turnaround time for the response to the RFP.

Wallace had a couple of questions. "Do you know anything about Advanced Technologies, Brian?"

"No, I don't. I was kind of hoping you might," Brian replied with a grin. "In any event, I do have their web address. Why don't you do a little research on these folks and see what you can find out."

"I'll do that," Wallace replied.

"Sounds good, and as soon as I have the RFP, I'll forward it to you. I think that your industry experience will serve us well on this one."

"I agree, Brian. I look forward to receiving the RFP. Talk with you later."

At 1:00 P.M., Brian checked his email and found that the RFP had yet to arrive, so he decided to spend a little time checking out AT's web site. Joe was right; the web site appeared dated. The site's latest news concerned SecureSoft's release more than 18 months earlier. Brian wondered whether or not this was the product that AT needed help marketing. In the event that it was, he decided to spend the 20 minutes before his next meeting gleaning information about SecureSoft from the web site.

After Brian returned to his desk from the meeting, he opened his email. The RFP had arrived 30 minutes earlier. He downloaded the five-page document and quickly scanned its content. His hunch was right. The product that AT was interested in aggressively marketing was in fact SecureSoft. Based on the information Brian found on the web site and in the RFP, the product looked to be interesting, possessing some potentially valuable features for commercial businesses interested in securing the content of their documents. Brian quickly composed an email to Wallace and attached the RFP for his review: Wallace opened the email within an hour of Brian's sending it. He quickly read the RFP, made some general notes, and then went back over it again to take more specific notes. Finally, he went through the document a third time, writing down questions that he thought to be relevant.

1. What is AT's revenue target for SecureSoft for the current fiscal year?
2. What are the anticipated unit sales?
3. What is the budgeted percent gross profit margin for the service offering?
4. What is AT's fiscal year timing?
5. Of the prospective buyers/decision makers that have been exposed to SecureSoft over the past 18 months, what has been their reaction?
6. Has product response been analyzed by industry or business vertical?
7. Has AT performed any form of competitive analysis to understand the SecureSoft's positioning in the field of other options?
8. Has the stated value proposition that appears in the RFP been used in any sales presentations or provided the foundation for communication points in any marketing materials? If yes, what has been the reaction of various audiences?
9. Who is the target audience and what issues can SecureSoft help them address?
10. What channels have been explored to sell and market SecureSoft? If some channels have been pursued, what are they, and what have been the results of these early efforts?
11. By what metrics will AT's management define SecureSoft's success?
12. How will AT define success?

After reviewing his list, Wallace decided to sleep on it and review it once more before sending it to Brian.

Wallace left the office at 6:00 P.M., thinking about the events of the day and the opportunity presented by AT. There were a lot of unknowns. The RFP provided some good background, but as Wallace contemplated the unanswered questions, he confronted big gaps that needed to be filled in order for GroupOne to come back with an intelligent proposal. It was important for him to get some answers concerning AT's greatest needs.

The next morning, Wallace arrived at the office at his usual time of 7:30. He walked down the hall to the office cafeteria, got himself a cup of coffee, and then returned to his desk. He reached in his desk drawer and pulled out the note pad that he was using to compose his thoughts on the key questions for AT. He reached for his pencil and jotted down Question 13:

> What are AT's greatest needs, which you expect to be addressed by the marketing services firm with which they partner?

Wallace read through his list of questions once more and made a couple of minor edits to the language. He then put the questions into a Word document that he attached to an email to Brian.

When Brian arrived at the office on Thursday morning at 8:30, he began the day as usual, turning on his computer, walking down the hall to grab a cup of tea from the cafeteria, and then returning to his desk to check his email. When he opened his email, he spied an email from Wallace with a subject line "Key Questions for AT." Wallace had done a great job of capturing the key questions that needed to be addressed. Brian placed a call to Wallace to let him know that he had received the email and would be forwarding the questions to the consultant. The phone rang twice before Wallace picked up. He could see that the call was coming from Brian's office.

"Good morning, Brian."

"Good morning, Wallace. Nice job on the questions for AT. I gave the RFP another read and, quite frankly, I'm not able to come up with anything to add to your list. I'm going to forward the list to Joe Albright this morning and check with him to see what time we'll be holding our conference call on Tuesday. Wallace, nice work! I'll let you know when I hear from Joe about our Tuesday call. Have a great day!"

"You too, Brian."

Brian composed an email and fired it off to Joe with the list of 13 questions attached. At the close of the email, he reminded Joe about the conference call on Tuesday and requested that Joe get back to him with a time for the call.

On Thursday morning just before noon, Joe opened his email and discovered Brian's message. He read the email and downloaded the Word document to review the questions. As he read the questions, he was struck by their strategic tone and quality of thought. He checked his calendar for next Tuesday and then sent Brian a response to set up a time for the conference call. Joe scheduled GroupOne's call for 11:30 A.M. and emailed Brian with the information.

Brian was in meetings all afternoon and did not check his email until he was ready to leave for the day. He opened his email and read Joe's message. He noted the suggested time for the call, checked his calendar and found that he was open at 11:30 A.M. He then checked the scheduling calendar for the office and found that Wallace was open for the call as well. Clicking on "Reply All," Brian forwarded a response to Joe to confirm the time of the call, copying Wallace on the reply.

The weekend passed. Prior to the Tuesday conference call, Brian thought it would be helpful to meet with Wallace once more to review the RFP and the questions they would be going over with Joe. Brian scheduled to meet Wallace at 3:00 P.M. Wallace arrived to the conference room at 3:00 P.M. sharp with Brian right behind him.

Brian began the meeting. "Wallace, how are you?"

"Great, Brian, and yourself?"

"Excellent. I'm feeling confident that we can be a huge help to the folks at AT."

"I agree, Brian. Based on the information in the RFP and the information that we were able to glean from the web site, it appears that AT has some pretty smart technology, but that they haven't been able to find a target audience or a compelling need that could be addressed by SecureSoft. I've also placed a few calls to some of my contacts in the software industry that work in data security. When I quizzed them on issues of document security, they told me that there are a number of players making claims similar to those of SecureSoft, but that no one, in their opinion, has cracked the code to capturing a lion's share of the market. Did you notice any serious gaps in the RFP with respect to background information or any other information?"

"Well, there were a couple of things I picked up on that I noted in my questions to AT. First, I think that we need to know how AT wants to promote itself in the current market and what success they've experienced with some of their early sales and marketing efforts. Given all the things that AT could and should be focusing on to effectively market their new product, I'd like to know what they've identified as their primary needs. If they want to achieve $2 million in sales within the first 12 months of the launch, I want to know the underlying issues and obstacles that are keeping them from achieving their goals."

"I'm with you, Wallace. When we have our call tomorrow morning with Joe, let's dig deep to get a sense of the obstacles to success from a sales and marketing perspective. Once we have that insight, we'll be in a better position to help AT. What else are we missing?"

"I think we should take a few moments to familiarize Joe with our closed-loop process for planning and program execution, because I think that it sets us apart from other agencies."

Brian liked where Wallace was heading. "I like your thoughts, Wallace. We'll make sure we hit on those points during the call. Anything else?"

"I can't think of anything," Wallace replied. "I look forward to the call."

"Me, too. Have a good evening."

"You do the same, Brian." As Wallace headed back to his desk, he felt fortunate to be working for an agency that appreciated his contributions and, moreover, to be working in an environment that valued teamwork.

The next morning, Joe was at his desk early, working on AT's sales plan. He took one more look at GroupOne's question list. As he reviewed the list, he was taken by the quality of the questions. The answers to these questions would clearly provide GroupOne with valuable strategic insight into AT's needs.

It was 11:30 A.M., and Brian and Wallace were dialing the conference bridge set up by Joe. Once they entered the pin number, the automated attendant requested the name of the conference call participant. "Brian Walker and Wallace Jones with GroupOne," Brian stated.

Joe was already on the line. "Brian and Wallace: How are you this morning?"

"Great, Joe, and you?" Brian replied.

"Couldn't be better, Brian," Wallace joined in.

"Brian," Joe continued, "I have your questions in front of me. How would you like to handle my responses? Do you want me to just go down the list as you presented them?"

"That would be great, Joe. Please, go ahead," Brian responded.

1. What is AT's revenue target for SecureSoft for the current fiscal year?

    "Well, we're putting together a business and sales plan as we speak. We've yet to nail down a hard number for anticipated revenues for this fiscal, but we'll refine our plan with the onboarding of our new head of sales and the marketing agency."

2. What are the anticipated unit sales?

    "The answer here is the same as with question one."

3. What is the budgeted percent gross profit margin for SecureSoft?

    "I can't tell you that definitively. Once we have the business plan put together along with the accompanying financials, we'll be able to share this information with you and the other agencies. Of course, that information, as well as the other information shared with you and the other agencies will be covered under the NDA that you've all signed."

"Okay, Joe," Brian chimed in. "How long before you have the first draft of your plan?"

"I plan on having it put together by next Wednesday, the date when the RFP responses will be due. Once we've narrowed the list of agencies down to two, we'll be sharing the draft of this plan with those agencies."

"Got it, Joe," Brian replied. "Next question."

4. What is AT's fiscal year timing?

    "This one I can answer in one breath," Joe laughed. "AT's fiscal year is the same as the calendar year."

Brian jumped in to help the Q&A process seem like less of an interrogation and more of a search by GroupOne for answers that would help frame its response to the RFP. "Joe, this is great. And, again, thanks for taking the time to go through these questions. Wallace and I are jotting down our notes as you speak. I realize that we have some questions that you can't answer yet, and I suspect that one of the reasons you reached out to our agency involves finding an agency that will assist in framing AT's future plans."

Brian thought it was a great time to introduce GroupOne's closed-loop approach to discovery, plan development, plan execution, measurement and analysis and refinement. Brian told Joe of how frequently GroupOne was called upon to assist its clients in facilitating and drafting an integrated sales and marketing plan, walking him through the steps of the process and then asking Wallace to describe a recent client engagement where he led the team through the process. Joe thanked Brian and Wallace for the overview, knowing that it was exactly what he wanted to see from a marketing services agency.

"Joe, whenever you're ready, please continue with the questions," said Brian.

5. Of the prospective buyers/decision makers that have been exposed to SecureSoft over the past 18 months, what has been their reaction?

> "This is a good question," Joe replied. "SecureSoft has been shared with approximately 20 businesses. These companies range in size from Fortune 1000 companies to a law firm with annual billings of $50 million dollars. The companies that have seen the product said nothing but positive things about it; yet, not a single prospect was willing to make a purchase. The reasons why they declined to buy ranged from the fact that the product was 'untested' in the marketplace to their not having the budget for the purchase. So, we need to understand the prospect need and how SecureSoft effectively addresses that need."

6. Has there been any analysis of the response to SecureSoft by industry or business vertical?

> "Not as of yet."

Joe considered responding further, but rather than giving another agency a tip on what he would like to see from an agency, he felt that he should let the statement stand and see how the various agencies responded to the data gaps in the SecureSoft plan.

7. Has AT performed any form of competitive analysis to understand SecureSoft's positioning in the field of other options?

> "Not as of yet. Once again, we felt that this was a great opportunity for the interested agencies to demonstrate how they could bring greater value to the relationship."

8. Has the stated value proposition that appears in the RFP been used in any sales presentations or provided the foundation for communications points in any marketing materials?

> "No, it hasn't. To be honest, management and I just put the UVP together last week in the course of a strategic planning session."

9. Who is the target audience and what issues can SecureSoft help them address?

> "Another good question. We're in the midst of working on this. Broadly stated, we believe that the target audience could be any company or business where documents and data are the lifeblood of the business."

10. What channels have been explored to sell and market SecureSoft? If some channels have been pursued, what are they, and what have been the results of these early efforts?

> "We believe that there are a number of channel opportunities to explore in addition to AT's own sales organization. However, as I already mentioned, we're in the midst of putting together our sales

Key Takeaways from Chapter 5

GroupOne's strategic approach to gaining insight into AT's business and marketing issues is critical to understanding AT's business needs. One of the areas of discovery was early customer reaction to the SecureSoft product. Additionally, analysis of SecureSoft's competitive challenges uncovered a need for AT to undertake both qualitative and quantitative primary market research. Serious questions existed relative to SecureSoft's positioning, pricing, and the terms and conditions of its sale. These issues are extremely common with any new product offering, but particularly for products that are paving new ground within new product categories, as is the case with SecureSoft.

Attempting to establish realistic goals for a new product without first exploring primary market research is a difficult process that rarely results in success. Although much can be said for making business judgments on one's "gut feelings," if a key executive first embarked on gaining marketplace intelligence, his or her judgment would be better placed and more effective.

Over time, successful consultants and business owners have learned crucial keys to business success: asking the right questions and listening carefully to the answers. Listening to current and prospective customers, as well as to the general marketplace brings a wealth of data upon which sound, effective business decisions can be made.

---

and marketing plan, so our channel options haven't been fully explored."

11. By what metrics will AT's management define SecureSoft's success?

    "One of the other agencies asked a similar question. Key measures of success for us will be market penetration and unit sales."

12. How will AT define success?

    "AT's founders would like to see the business generate $2 MM in revenues in the first 12 months and reach $4 million in sales by the third year."

13. Describe as specifically as you can AT's greatest needs, which you expect to be addressed by the marketing services firm that you partner with.

    "AT has a couple of sizeable obstacles. The first is the lack of a strong and experienced sales executive. This is a position that AT is presently in the market to fill. The second is the lack of a well-conceived marketing plan and a marketing team to execute that plan. AT has initiated this RFP process to find a marketing services agency that can step up to the challenge to effectively become the marketing department for AT."

Joe asked if there were any additional questions.

"I don't think so, Joe," replied Brian. "I think that you answered all of our questions and we understand that there are still answers to come based on the development of your sales and marketing plans. Based on the timeline that you've set forth for the RFP process, we need to have our response to you by next Wednesday, and we'll begin working on that response today. Wallace will be our point person on developing the response."

Brian thought the timing was right to bring the conference call to a close. "Joe, I guess that does it for us for right now. Did you have anything more for us at this point?"

"No, not right now. I look forward to seeing your response to the RFP. If you more questions, give me a call or drop me an email."

The conference call was brought to a close. After Joe hung up the phone, he sat back in his chair and reflected on the conference call. GroupOne was obviously not a run-of-the-mill agency. They demonstrated great thought quality and sincere interest in addressing AT's sales and marketing issues.

GroupOne learned early on that their success in solving sales and marketing problems for their clients would come from a clear understanding of their clients' business dynamics, which came in part from insight derived from asking the "right" questions of the "right" audiences. The probing business questions put to AT helped uncover the issues that needed to be addressed in order to execute a well-conceived sales and marketing plan. Furthermore, asking the right questions of the customers and prospective customers would help identify the market need for a solution like SecureSoft. If the process were done properly, AT would undertake both qualitative and quantitative research among customers and prospects to properly assess the needs of the marketplace and the value of AT's technology. At the end of the day, research done right spawns an accurate assessment of market needs and interests.

GroupOne distinguished themselves from the other agencies by asking legitimately intelligent questions of AT, such that, in the early stages of the selling process, they were able to accomplish two critical points of competitive advantage: They set themselves apart from the other agencies by displaying strategic insight into AT's needs, which therefore put GroupOne in a better position to frame an effective response to AT's RFP. In the early steps of the selling process, this was a key win for GroupOne.

6
AT's Customer Buying Process

After conducting the conference calls on Monday, Joe spent Tuesday and Wednesday reflecting on each agency's response. Given the quality of their strategic thinking and intuitive questions, GroupOne stood out from the other agencies. Their questions caused Joe to reflect a little deeper on AT's needs and how he could better communicate these needs to a marketing services agency.

Joe studied GroupOne's web site and was impressed with the methodologies that were presented there. They had some excellent process elements that helped him understand their thinking regarding customer acquisition, and he knew that GroupOne's model of the customer buying process would be helpful in defining AT's agency selection process. On a page entitled "Customer Buying Process," Joe found a diagram (Exhibit 6-1) with a comprehensive portrayal of the process.

Exhibit 6-1. Customer Buying Process

Joe liked how each step was sequenced and outlined within the *process*. The customer buying process had been depicted by the other experts and business gurus, but not in the form of a continuous closed-loop process, which highlighted the interlocking relationship of each step with the others. During the process of addressing a single customer need, new needs typically arise, and GroupOne's diagram made it easy to trace the origin and anticipate the solution to these needs. When Joe and the Scotts conducted their strategic planning session, they analyzed the steps of the customer buying process to understand the thought process of prospective customers, but they documented the process hierarchically, not homogeneously. GroupOne's process diagram made up for this by portraying the steps interdependently.

Joe pulled out a note pad and began making notes. Because AT had already recognized a need, which meant that there was no issue with problem recognition, he skipped over the first step of the customer buying process and moved to the second step, labeling it a little differently than GroupOne had.

What is the Need?

As he reflected on this question, he thought about AT's sales and marketing needs. AT had done little to formalize a sales process for the introduction of SecureSoft and little more to formalize SecureSoft's value proposition beyond what Joe and the Scotts had put together in their planning session. Like many bright software developers, the Scotts had created an amazing application, but they lacked the sales and marketing expertise to effectively launch it. To stimulate sales for SecureSoft, they needed a higher level of sales and marketing support. AT's role of marketing in support of the sales process was ill defined, but the Scotts were willing to let Joe and the forthcoming marketing agency devise a plan that defined specific roles and responsibilities.

How will the Need be Satisfied?

Understanding how a product will satisfy customer needs is imperative to building customer confidence. To be confident in making a purchase, an intelligent buyer needs to understand a product or service's approach to addressing identified needs, which made it crucial for AT to understand how each potential marketing agency would help market SecureSoft.

AT's management needed to know exactly what steps would be taken to meet the company's revenue goals for the next 12 months. What strategy would provide the "road map" to success? What mixture of marketing tactics would the marketing agency deploy? What role would database marketing play? AT had not developed a prospect database. If they pursued direct marketing, what criteria would be used to develop the list source strategy?

In addition to overseeing the agency search, Joe was in the process of composing AT's sales and marketing plan. He and the Scotts had already identified seven logical verticals to pursue: accounting, architects, legal, banking, healthcare services, healthcare insurance, and financial investment services. At this point, however, the plan was fairly skeletal, and Joe needed a marketing agency to help him put flesh to the bones. Once the marketing plan was outlined, he would also need help detailing a comprehensive tactical plan. What would be the role of e-communications via the web and email marketing? What role would direct mail play? What role would traditional print advertising play? Should AT participate in trade shows? If so, which shows and how would the trade show planning and execution process be managed? How would the trade show events fit in with other lead generation/demand generation programs?

Joe had been reading business articles on demand generation and felt that SecureSoft was a great candidate for a targeted demand generation program. Beyond tactics and strategy, Joe was interested to see each agency's conception of a detailed measurement and tracking plan—a plan that identified effective tactics for achieving stated objectives.

Another important dimension in AT's marketing mix was the Internet. Joe had read a few articles on Search Engine Optimization (SEO) and Pay Per Click (PPC) campaigns, but he was unsure about how to capitalize on these marketing tools. How would SEO, Paid Advertising and social media such as Facebook, LinkedIn and Twitter fit into the marketing mix? The more he read, the more convinced Joe became that prospective customers who were in the early stages of the buying process would be doing the majority of their research on the Internet. He recalled one article that he read that indicated that better than 80 percent of the B2B market across all product and service categories were doing some form of research on the Internet before making a purchase. It was intuitive to believe that prospective customers for SecureSoft would look to the Internet to research their options and become better educated on document security issues long before they discovered SecureSoft. In fact, given other, more pressing issues in their businesses, AT's prospects might not even recognize that they have a data security issue, meaning that AT would need to be vigilant about educating SecureSoft's prospect universe on data security needs and data security solutions. Feeling comfortable with his knowledge of the third step in the customer buying process, Joe moved on to the fourth step.

Who Is Involved in the Process?

As he considered the process of identifying and securing the best marketing agency for AT, Joe tore off a new sheet from his note pad and made two columns. He titled the first column "AT" and the second column "Marketing Agency". In the AT column, he listed the Scotts and himself as the key stakeholders in the decision-making process. In the marketing agency column, he listed the titles of individuals that he believed would be critically involved in various stages of the buying and selling process:

- VP of Sales (Business Development)
- VP or Director of Client Services
- Account Executive

Then, considering relationship development and agency assessment, he added another title, president or CEO. Although it was not a necessary point of contact in every B2B relationship, Joe felt that, given the size of the agency that AT would be dealing with and the account size that AT could represent to them, a senior executive within the agency needed to be at the table. Joe wanted to be certain that the agency had commitment from the very top, and he was confident that the Scotts would agree. If the president or CEO were not interested in committing time to developing a relationship with AT, AT should not be interested in forming a relationship with the agency.

Evaluating Our Options

AT had identified four prospective marketing agencies, each of which would soon be presenting what they believed was the best solution for AT. Yet just one agency would be selected. Working through the process of agency selection, Joe felt that a scorecard would ensure that AT was both consistent and comprehensive in its approach to selecting the best agency. Joe finalized the selection criteria, using each criterion as a tool for uniformly assessing each agency.

Exhibit 6-2. AT's Agency Scorecard

Criteria	Weighting	Score (1-5 w/ 5=outstanding)	Total
1. Industry experience	7		
2. Agency size	6		
3. Agency years in business	5		
4. Proposal cost vs. services delivered	8		
5. Financial stability	8		
6. Percent client retention	8		
7. Senior management commitment	11		
8. Caliber of the team assigned to the business	12		
9. Caliber of references of existing and prior clients	15		
10. Demonstrated expertise in managing fully integrated marketing mix elements e.g. print, direct mail, telemarketing, email, web (SEO, PPC, Internet marketing)	20		
Total	100		

Based on the weighting, a perfect score would be 500 points. Joe felt that "demonstrated expertise" was the most important criterion, allocating it 20 percent weighting, followed by 15 percent for "caliber of references" and 12 percent for the "caliber of the team" that would be assigned to work with AT on a day-to-day basis. As he looked through the criteria a second and third time, he was surprised that he had weighted "proposal cost vs. services delivered" at 8percent. Yet, the more he thought about it, the more convinced he became that weighting it at 8% was indeed appropriate. AT was most interested in the "thought value" they would receive from an agency. AT had a limited budget, but, as long as costs were in the realm of reasonableness, Joe believed that the key to selecting an agency would hinge more on the other criteria. He emailed the scorecard to Frank and Marlie to get their input.

Frank and Marlie were at their desks when Joe's email came through. They read it within five minutes of each other. After reading Joe's cover message, the Scotts opened the scorecard and quickly scanned the criteria.

"Marlie, did you open this email from Joe Albright yet?"

"Yes, I did. What are your thoughts?" asked Marlie.

"I like it a lot. I think he's captured the key criteria. We can debate some of the weightings, but, directionally, I think he's right on." Frank turned in his chair to face Marlie's desk. "What do you think?"

"I agree with you," she replied. "I really like the idea of having a consistent approach and process to evaluate these agencies. I think we need to take as much subjectivity out of our decision-making process as possible, and I think this helps. I also like the weighting element. I think it's fair to state that not all characteristics carry the same level of importance. This framework does a nice job of placing emphasis on critical characteristics while not neglecting the others. This is a very smart tool. Do you want to reply to Joe or should I?"

"I'll reply," said Frank, and fired off an email to Joe indicating their approval of the scorecard.

GroupOne's proposal to AT was due in one week, and Brian Walker needed to update Paul Austin on GroupOne's opportunity with AT. He walked down the hall to Paul's office. As always, the door was open.

"Hey Paul, you got a minute?"

"Sure, Brian. What's up?"

Brian paused to collect his thoughts. "Well, I just wanted to tell you that Wallace is putting together a response to an RFP from a company named Advanced Technologies, which they'll receive by next Tuesday."

"Okay. What's the opportunity?"

Brian was hesitant to go into detail about AT, but he wanted to prepare Paul for the possibility of being asked to participate in a client presentation.

"Advanced Technologies is a small, well-funded software development firm that has recently released a new application that secures data files of all types when transmitted over the Internet," Brian replied. "The owners have approached a total of four marketing services agencies. I can't tell you the size of the account yet, but

I think it's safe to say that it will be a low six figures, somewhere in the neighborhood of $150K to $200K, annualized."

Paul's interest was piqued. "How did they hear about us?"

"The company hired a consultant named Joe Albright to put together an RFP and send it out to the agencies. I know he spent some time getting recommendations from his network and doing Internet research."

Brian took the opportunity to praise the work that GroupOne had done since Stephanie Atwood became VP of Marketing & Strategy Development. "Paul, I have to tell you, the work that Stephanie and her team have been doing to improve our web presence has been paying dividends. This is the fourth new opportunity that's come our way this month and each of the prospective clients has been well qualified."

"That's great. I hope you've shared that appreciation with Stephanie and her team."

"I have. Back to Advanced Technologies, based on the conversation that we had yesterday with their consultant, Joe Albright, I think that we have a good shot at this one. My sense is that, if we're called in as one of the last two agencies, it would be valuable to have you in on the presentation."

"I'd love to Brian. Just let me know when, and I'll block the time on my calendar."

"This should move fairly quickly," Brian responded, "but we probably won't receive word from the consultant for at least a week following the deadline for the responses. So, I likely won't get back to you before a week from next Wednesday. But I'll keep you posted."

"Sounds good, Brian."

"I hope we win this one. I'll talk with you later."

"Have a good one, Brian," Paul replied as Brian left his office.

Brian was headed back to his office when he turned back down the hall to touch bases with Wallace. "Hey, Wallace. How's it going?"

"Great, Brian. How about you?"

"I'm good. Have you made any headway on the response to the AT RFP?"

"Yes, I have. I've called a team meeting with Stephanie and Susan for this afternoon at 3:30," Wallace replied. "Would you like to join in?"

"No, I know that you can handle it on your own; unless, that is, you'd like my involvement."

"Well, I didn't send you a meeting invite because I thought you had a lot going on, and I think I've got a good handle on what we need to do. I just thought it might be smart to consult the account services folks at this early stage, and Stephanie is always a good one to make a contribution to the marketing strategy elements of a response," Wallace replied.

"I think you've got enough brain power in the meeting already, but call me if you have a question I can answer."

"Will do, Brian. Thanks for stopping by."

"Sure thing, Wallace. Have a good one."

Across town, Joe was busy working on AT's sales and marketing plan outline.

Based on the results of the strategic planning session, he predicted the dollar target for SecureSoft, but his thoughts were focused mainly on developing SecureSoft's promotional, advertising, PR, and channeling strategies. Inasmuch as he felt that it was important for the incoming sales executive to participate in the planning process, he knew that, if he had a rough plan put together before the executive came on board, the agency would not waste valuable time on plan design. Most importantly, a majority of time and effort should be dedicated to gaining a clear understanding of the AT business, its customers and prospective customers, and focusing on the *execution* of a sales and marketing plan.

The core plan was near completion. Joe spent several more hours performing data analysis of the vertical industry segments previously defined as high-potential verticals for SecureSoft.

On Wednesday, with the plan 90 percent complete, Joe took a break from writing. He could wrap it up on Thursday and still beat the deadline that he and the Scotts had set in their strategic planning session.

Although he had already researched the four prospective agencies on the Internet, Joe decided to revisit their respective web sites and associated links. First, he reviewed The Foster Group's site. He was unimpressed. Most of the content appeared dated, with the most recent posting to the "current events" page being three months old. And when he reviewed the client list, he found only one client associated with the high-tech verticals. Digging deeper, Joe followed several links under the menu tab, "case studies." Strangely, the links that included client logos only connected to the client's home page instead of connecting to pages that referenced the work of The Foster Group.

To test the quality of The Foster Group's web marketing, Joe entered keywords from The Foster Group's web site into Google and Yahoo. He was surprised to see that the company was not listed within the first six search citations. In fact, he had to go five pages deep before he found a reference to The Foster Group. To Joe, it was a sign that the agency was not practicing what it preached.

Next, Joe visited the web site for Slone Direct. Slone had been in business for 10 years and was a fairly well-respected direct marketing agency. He had heard some good things about Slone from his network, but he wanted to get a closer impression of their capabilities with respect to Internet marketing and strategy development. When he landed on the site, he was instantly turned off. The images focused almost entirely on direct mail. There were references to other elements of the marketing mix, including the Internet, Email marketing and alternative media, but, visually, the content was not effectively communicated. Joe spent some time examining the owners' biographies. Their credentials were impressive, and the agency's awards were impressive as well. However, most of the awards related to direct marketing, specifically direct mail. Joe was disconcerted to find no references to Slone's strategic consulting services. AT would be relying on a marketing agency to provide analytic and strategic development services, for there were few resources in these areas of expertise at AT.

As he had done with The Foster Group, Joe searched Google and Yahoo using keywords from the company's web site. Slone Direct failed to appear in the first half dozen search references, which, again, insinuated incompetence in Internet marketing.

Having already spent time at GroupOne's web site, Joe decided to revisit MarCom's site. Upon arriving at MarCom.com, Joe immediately lowered the volume on his computer speakers to dampen the site's loud, synthesized mood music. After clicking on a few media files, he found an interesting video where an attractive young woman spoke about the importance of integrated communications, whether delivered through the Internet, direct mail, email, print advertising, or other forms of marketing communication. The spokeswoman then invited the visitor to spend time reviewing MarCom's marketing services.

Perusing the site further, Joe discovered an opportunity to download a whitepaper concerning demand generation. He began filling in the required information fields, which requested more data than he felt was necessary, such as his company address, his title and his phone number. But he wanted to get a look at the paper's content. Unfortunately, the paper was just three pages long and contained no case studies, just jargon and generalized business tips that were useless to composing a refined marketing plan.

Repeating his Google and Yahoo searches for MarCom, Joe found the agency's first citation on page two of the search results. Again, this was not a demonstration of Internet marketing prowess, but it was better than the previous two agencies. Joe returned to Google and typed in a few more keywords and phrases from MarCom's site, but, again, found no first page citations.

Finally, Joe decided to take a second look at GroupOne's web site. He was once more impressed with the site's clear, clean look. It was rich in content yet easy to navigate. When Joe revisited the "client experience" page, he found multiple case studies available for download. Of the four agencies that he was considering, only GroupOne offered case study downloads.

After clicking the download button, an access form requesting only Joe's first and last name, company name and email address appeared, which made his privacy feel less invaded. After reading the summaries of three case studies, he downloaded two that appeared relevant to AT's situation.

Like the web site's other written content, the case studies were crisp and concise. Joe valued how the statement of a client's objectives was coupled with GroupOne's strategy to meet the objectives, and both case studies addressed integrated tactics deployed in marketing initiatives with great specificity. The ROMI for both clients was impressive. In the first case study, the client broke even on their planned 12-month marketing investment within the first 90 days of the campaign launch; and at the end of the first 12 months, they realized a 300 percent ROMI.

As he had done with the other agencies, Joe conducted Google and Yahoo searches using key words from GroupOne's site. Impressively, GroupOne not only showed up within the top five citations on the first page of the search, but it had invested in Pay Per Click searches with both Yahoo and Google. In Joe's assessment,

Key Takeaways from Chapter 6

Decision-Making Scorecard—Joe Albright's creation of a "scorecard" to evaluate the agencies competing for AT's business is not unique. But it does point out the value of first identifying the most important criteria for judging agencies. Additionally, recognizing that not all of the criteria were ultimately of equal value makes an important point about distinguishing elements that represent the greatest value in the ultimate decision. Scorecards such as the one illustrated in this chapter can be used in a multitude of ways. Whenever faced with a major decision, it can be helpful to breakdown the key elements to consider when making the decision. For example, when considering a job or a career change, think about the number of factors beyond salary that would be important to consider in the decision, and, as in the case of the AT scorecard, placing a weight on each of the criteria will balance the elements in the final analysis.

Internet Marketing—As illustrated in this chapter, whether a business model is B2B or B2C, it is imperative that sufficient time and resources are put toward making a company web site easily found. Some Internet marketing experts suggest that, if a search of common "keywords" related to a product or service fails to show up above the search's fold, the company is missing out on business opportunity. Today's common practice of first turning to the Internet to research a topic, a service or a product means that failure to have sufficient presence within the key search engines (Google, Yahoo, AOL, & Bing) is to miss out on the early stages of the customer buying process. A business is wise to make the necessary investment in time and expert resources to ensure a solid performance in search engine rankings. In addition, given the continuing growth of social media, taking time to make certain that your business has a well-thought out social media strategy within relevant media channels (e.g. Facebook, Twitter, LinkedIn, YouTube) will go a long way toward driving greater success.

---

this was a sign of competent Internet marketing and was another high mark for GroupOne.

Joe was anxious to see how each agency responded to the RFP. Yet, if the conference calls and the experience listed on the agencies respective web sites were an indication, GroupOne would be tough to beat. As Joe reflected on his comfort level with each agency, he felt that his decision was already made. In any event, one thing was certain: At that early stage in the process, GroupOne was the superior agency.

7
The Perfect Selling Process

It was Thursday morning, and the GroupOne team had just four working days to finalize their response to AT's RFP. On Wednesday, Wallace had a productive internal planning session with Susan and Stephanie. They brainstormed and came up with creative solutions that could successfully launch SecureSoft. Keeping in mind AT's customer buying process, Wallace used GroupOne's "Enterprise Selling Process" model (Exhibit 7-1) to keep the team focused as they moved forward.

Exhibit 7-1. Enterprise Selling Process

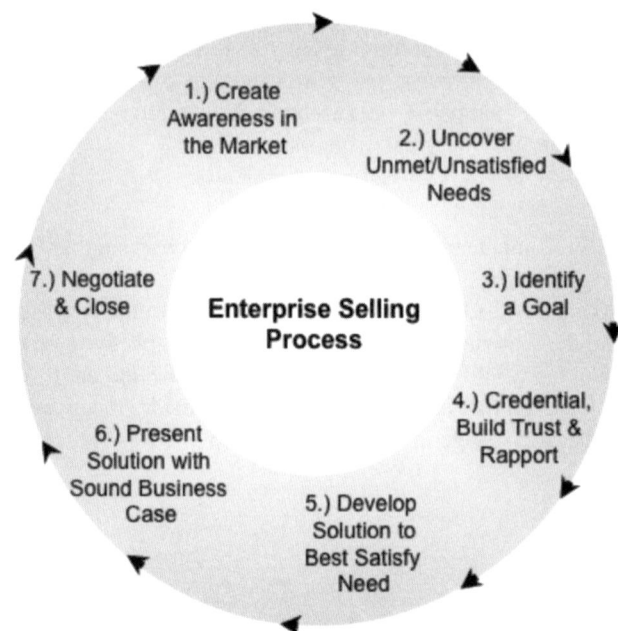

Based on the information provided by the RFP and conference call, GroupOne had a good handle on AT's business goals. Coming out of the RFP planning session with Susan and Stephanie, Wallace crafted goal statements supported by strategy statements. Once tactics were applied and executed, Wallace was confident that GroupOne would be in a position to help AT achieve its qualitative and quantitative goals.

QUALITATIVE GOALS:

Introduce and sell SecureSoft to a targeted universe of business decision makers.

QUANTITATIVE GOALS:

1. Generate a minimum of $1 million in revenues in the first 12 months with average revenue per new customer of $36,000.
2. Double the customer base in the second and third years to realize a $4 million business at the end of three years, retaining 95% of the customer base from year to year.

The goals called for a highly integrated multistage, multichannel strategy. Such an approach would entail the use of traditional direct mail, email, web content, outbound calling, traditional print advertising in trade magazines, and PR strategies. The terms *multistage* and *multichannel* were new to the marketing lexicon. *Multistage* refers to the communications that take place in the various stages of the buying process. The strategy recognizes the reality of how buyers make decisions and how they secure information to make their decisions. In a multistage contact strategy, various communications take place between the seller and the prospective customer to continuously build on the selling enterprise's unique value proposition, which allows the seller further insight into the specific needs of the prospective customer. Over time, the multistage approach intends to marry the customer's needs with the seller's unique value proposition, resulting in a sale.

The term *multichannel* communicates the fact that prospective customers rely on various sources or "channels" of communication to perform research on a product prior to making a buying decision. Some company decision makers prefer to receive product information through direct mail and email, while others prefer sourcing their information by Internet or telephone. In any case, successful sellers tailor their sales approach around these preferences to insure that they reach the "right" people with the "right" message at the "right" time through the "right" channel, as portrayed by GroupOne.

Upon examining AT's business approach, GroupOne discovered that AT had not formally researched SecureSoft's potential value to its prospective customers. Both Wallace and Stephanie felt strongly that, before AT invested significant money in tactical marketing initiatives, AT should invest in qualitative research (focus groups) followed by quantitative research (surveys) to fine-tune its marketing strategies and key communications elements. Not only would the research provide a clearer understanding of SecureSoft's unique value proposition; it would provide an effective means for profiling and segmenting SecureSoft's prospect universe. Segmentation research would be helpful in gaining insight into the attitudinal segments that existed within the prospect universe, which would help fine-tune the messaging for product attributes that appealed to the segments. GroupOne had considerable experience helping clients discover opportunities to both improve the features of new products and develop refined marketing strategies for the products, and a client's investing money upfront on market research had consistently proven invaluable to improving the quality and effectiveness of its tactical marketing initiatives.

Brian visited Wallace to see how he was progressing on the response to AT's RFP. "Hey, Wallace. How's it going?"

"Hi, Brian. I'm pretty far along in putting our response together for AT. Stephanie and Susan were extremely helpful in our meeting yesterday. Right now, Susan is pulling together some relevant case studies to include in the response."

"Sounds like you're making great progress," Brian commented.

"I think we are, Brian. My plan is to have a full draft completed by tomorrow, so we can have the weekend to review it. Then we can make any revisions on Monday and have the response out the door on Tuesday . . . one day in advance of the due date."

"That's great, Wallace. I look forward to seeing the draft tomorrow. I was also thinking that it might be good for either you or I to call Joe Albright to give him an update on our progress and to see if there's any additional information that he'd like to pass along."

"Well, I'm pretty buried in preparing this response, and I think that a call coming from you would demonstrate senior management interest. What do you think?"

"I agree. I'll make the call this afternoon. Are there any additional questions that you'd like for me to ask Joe?"

"I don't think so. I think we're pretty well set. Actually, there's one more thing that I'd like to know."

"Sure, what is it?"

"When I went over our questions and the questions asked by the competing agencies, I didn't see any requests for copies of primary research that AT had undertaken on SecureSoft. Does any quantitative or qualitative research exist?"

"I don't know. That's a good question. I'll ask Joe. Any other thoughts?"

"No, I think that does it." Brian complimented Wallace on his progress and headed back to his office.

At 2:00 P.M. on Thursday, Brian placed the call to Joe Albright. The phone rang half a dozen times and then went to voice mail, where Brian left the following message. "Hi, Joe. It's Brian Walker with GroupOne. I'm calling to touch base with you about the preparation of the RFP response. I have a few quick questions to ask you. Please get back to me at your convenience and have a great day." Brian then began responding to some emails.

An hour later, Brian got a call from GroupOne's receptionist, Cynthia. "Brian, you have a call from Joe Albright on line one."

"Thanks, Cynthia. Hey, Joe. Thanks for getting back to me."

"No problem, Brian. How can I help you?"

"Well, I just wanted to let you know that we've had some internal meetings in preparation for our response to you. At this point, we're on schedule to send our response by the end of Tuesday. But, as we were going through your company information along with your responses to our conference call questions, we didn't find a reference to primary research that AT had undertaken prior to launching SecureSoft."

"Thanks for the update on your progress. As for primary research, AT hasn't conducted any formal research. They've obtained prospective customers' reactions to SecureSoft, but those comments haven't been documented. For the most part, the feedback has been anecdotal. We've talked about the value of doing some research, but we didn't want to make a big financial commitment right off of the bat."

"I can appreciate that, but, if you're open to the recommendation, we'd like to at least incorporate some focus groups and possibly follow that qualitative research with a larger survey that would help us profile and segment the prospect universe."

"That's fine, Brian, but just know that we don't have unlimited funds, and, the more we spend on research, the less we have for marketing tactics."

"I understand. For the past several years, we've been working with a small research outfit on projects of your size and we've come up with some very cost effective solutions for developing marketing insight."

"That sounds great, Brian. I'll leave the matter up to you and your team, but I'd like to see the cost associated with the research presented separately."

"You bet, Joe. As a general practice, our proposals include a detailed line item budget along with a tactical implementation timeline. That way, we can have a conversation about what we want to eliminate, add, or expand in the plan. Is there anything else that you'd like to share with me at this time?"

"No, not right now. Thanks for checking in with me, though."

"My pleasure, Joe. If something comes up don't hesitate to give me a call or drop me an email. We look forward to giving you our response next Tuesday."

"Thanks again for the call, Brian. Talk with you later."

After ending his call with Joe, Brian immediately called Wallace. "Wallace, it's Brian. I just got off of the phone with Joe Albright. AT hasn't conducted formal research on SecureSoft. They've made presentations to a few prospective customers and received some feedback, but nothing's been documented. You should probably have a conversation with Stephanie to get her thoughts on incorporating qualitative and quantitative research in our response."

"Sounds good, Brian. I'll contact Stephanie right away. Anything else?"

"No, that's pretty much it. I did tell Joe that we were on pace to get him the response by the close of business on Tuesday. Does that timing still work for you?"

"Yes, it does, and thanks for keeping me updated."

"No problem, Wallace. Have a good afternoon."

"You too, Brian."

After hanging up with Brian, Wallace called Stephanie. "Stephanie, it's Wallace."

"Hi, Wallace. How's it going with the RFP response?"

"It's going well. That's actually why I'm calling. I just got off the phone with Brian. He was talking with Joe Albright and learned that AT hadn't performed market research on their new product outside of fielding the opinions of a few prospective customers. He suggested that I give you a call to see if we can incorporate a recommendation for research in our proposal."

"I'd be happy to work on it, Wallace. I can probably have some recommendations to you by tomorrow."

For the last ten years, GroupOne had worked closely with Al and Nancy Lungren of The Lungren Group, a small, highly specialized marketing research firm located just three miles down the road from GroupOne. The Lungrens had more than 50 years of experience in designing and executing qualitative and quantitative research for companies with either a business-to-business (B2B) model or a business-to-consumer (B2C) model. Because of their low overhead, the Lundgrens consistently delivered quality research solutions at below traditional market prices.

Stephanie gave Al and Nancy a call. "Hi, Nancy. It's Stephanie at GroupOne. How are you today?"

"Great, Stephanie. How about you?"

"I'm fine. Thanks for asking. I'm calling regarding a proposal that we're working on for a prospective client. Do you have a couple of minutes?"

"Sure, Stephanie. What's going on?"

Stephanie proceeded to familiarize Nancy with GroupOne's opportunity with AT and then turned to the issue of market research. "Now that you understand our position with AT, could you and Al develop a methodology that provides insight for a profiling and segmentation analysis along with an approach that would help us uncover the attributes and characteristics that potential customers would find valuable in SecureSoft?"

"Sure, we can do that. When do you need to see something from us?"

"You're going to feel like shooting me for this, but can you just sketch out your thoughts with some ballpark estimates and have something to me by tomorrow?"

"Sure. It may be late tomorrow, but we can make it happen."

"Great, Nancy. I really appreciate this. I owe you big time."

"Don't be too hasty. You haven't seen what we're delivering yet." Nancy and Stephanie shared a laugh.

"Is there anything else, Stephanie?"

"No, that's it. And, again, thanks for pushing this through so quickly. Let's find a time to get together next week."

"Sounds good, Stephanie. Next Thursday or Friday would be good for us."

"How about lunch on Friday?"

"That works for us. Let's meet at 11:45 at the Stonebridge Café."

"Perfect, Nancy. I'll see you on Friday, and I'll look forward to receiving your recommendations tomorrow."

As Stephanie was ending her call, Wallace was at his desk putting together some additional thoughts for the AT response. Susan had just sent him four case studies concerning work that GroupOne had performed for clients in three different verticals: two in high-tech, one in financial services, and one in the health care sector. One of the high-tech case studies involved a client that Wallace had worked with, but he was unfamiliar with the high-tech client in the other study. Thinking that Molly McBride may have handled the project, he got up from his desk and walked over to see if Molly was in. "Hey, Molly. You got a minute?"

"Sure, Wallace. What's up?"

"I'm responding to an RFP from a company named Advanced Technologies."

"Yes, Brian mentioned that you were working on that opportunity. How can I help you?"

"Well, Susan sent me four case studies, and I'm familiar with three of them, but I'm not familiar with the work that GroupOne did for *this* client." Wallace put the case study in front of Molly to see if she recognized it.

"Yes, I remember this client. I brought them to GroupOne about two years ago. Like AT, they develop and market commercial software solutions for businesses. When they contacted us, the client thought that they had a tiger by the tail in an application that they'd developed for the accounting industry. The application was geared toward privately held small to mid-size companies. The application had a module that helped with estate and succession planning. Its selling point was a tax module that helped the client minimize the tax burden on the business when new family members took over. Would you like to hear what we did for the company?"

"If you can spare the time, that would be great," Wallace replied.

"No problem. Have a seat and I'll take you through the process that we took the client through."

Molly started from the beginning. "As I mentioned earlier, the client came to us two years ago. They learned about us from our web site and then checked in with a few of our clients. My first conversation was with the co-founder of the business. He and his partner had been in the accounting business for over a decade. I asked him some basic questions about his business to get an idea of the challenges he was facing. Then, I asked the co-founder and his partner what they wanted to achieve in terms of sales. He and his partner lacked sales and marketing expertise, and they didn't employ business development people. In fact, they hadn't conducted any marketing research, which told me that we were starting from square one. So, we agreed to have a planning meeting where we mapped out marketing and sales objectives."

Molly sipped her tea and continued. "Stephanie joined me in the meeting, and our first order of business was defining the product's unique value proposition, which we based on the gut intuition of the company's owners. After we went through the exercise, we came to an agreement that, in order to best position the product, we needed to perform primary market research. So, I volunteered to help put together a research plan. Once we completed the research, we were able to refine the UVP. Our next step was defining the client's business objectives. Based on their exposure to a large number of prospects through accounting relationships, we were able to define expected unit sales for the first 12 months. Not much thought had been given to pricing strategies, so we came up with revenue targets for year one. Then, I suggested that, once we had some solid data in hand, we should develop the brand messaging and determine the strategies and tactics we'd use to heighten awareness in the prospect universe."

Wallace was impressed with Molly and Stephanie's approach. In essence, GroupOne outlined the entire strategic business/marketing plan for the client.

"The next step," Molly continued, "was to outline the process for lead generation, qualification and nurturing. Today, that process is usually referred to as demand generation or demand creation. The difference between lead generation and demand generation is that, in lead generation, we assume that there's a pent-up demand in the marketplace for a product or service, while in demand generation, the assumption is that the target audience isn't fully aware of the need for a product or service. In the case of this service, we could safely assume that a latent need really existed, which meant that we were dealing with demand generation, which is more complex than it sounds. The client had to think about how to create product awareness and educate prospective clients on the value of addressing estate and succession planning issues. Because the company didn't have a sales force or a business development person, the owners decided to hire a sales professional. Once they hired the sales professional, GroupOne worked with him to define the characteristics of a qualified lead, one that had a clear business issue that could be addressed by the software solution. One of the first things we did was define the firmographics of the prospect universe; from here, we developed a list source strategy. Next, we created a prospective client database, and after that we developed and executed a plan to heighten awareness in the marketplace, which identified prospects that had a real need for the software. Because not all prospects are ready to buy when an enterprise is ready to sell, we put together a plan that constantly nurtured the businesses in the prospect database. When the need arose for our client's solution, an awareness of the solution was well established. We also worked closely with the client's sales team to develop a sales plan and steps in the selling process. In the end," Molly concluded, "I would say that the unique aspect of our work was the fact that our efforts were geared toward making the salesperson's job as easy as possible, from the development of the product positioning to the creation of product awareness in the marketplace. Ultimately, it's not about printing up pretty brochures; it's about sales and marketing working together to create sales."

"Your explanation really helps, but I have one question."

"What's that?"

"What were the results of these efforts?"

"I was wondering if you were going to ask," Molly smiled. "Truth be told, the actual results are understated in this case study. Not only did we exceed the year one revenue and unit objectives, but our client added an additional module to the package six months into the year, and, by year's end, 40 percent of the predicted customer base purchased the expanded package, making the return on marketing investment in excess of 300 percent. Every dollar invested in the marketing and sales initiative generated three dollars of net operating profit in the first 12 months. As a result, we've retained this client for over two years."

"Very impressive. Thanks again for taking the time to share this with me. The similarities to AT's circumstances are very close. Well, I better get back to writing the response to the RFP. Once again, thanks for the help."

"You're welcome, Wallace, and good luck with this opportunity. GroupOne has a great story to tell. Now all you need to do is go tell it!"

Wallace got up from his chair and checked his watch. It was 5:15 P.M., but he felt that he should spend another couple of hours crafting the response while Molly's story was fresh in his mind. He felt that GroupOne's approach to the client in the case study would be a perfect approach for communicating a sales and marketing framework to AT.

Instead of producing pages upon pages of prose, Wallace decided to explain the sales and marketing process in simple straightforward terms. He felt that a simple, uncomplicated approach would best communicate how sales and marketing needed to work hand in hand to achieve marketing success. Referring to his notes from his meeting with Molly, Wallace laid out the following process steps:

1. Define marketplace opportunity.
2. Develop brand positioning and awareness.
3. Address demand generation and product nursing.
4. Chart sales opportunity development.
5. Accomplish sales closure.
6. Foster customer relationship development.

As Wallace went back over his notes, the process became increasingly clear. It was easy to see how the first three steps were almost entirely owned by marketing. Yet, as he reflected on his own experience, he saw how sales could offer valuable contributions to the first three steps. Conversely, even though sales had ownership of the last three steps, he saw how marketing should have a role in contributing to "opportunity development," as well as closing the sale and developing long-standing customer relationships. The interrelationship of sales and marketing in the sales and marketing process was an epiphany for Wallace, and he felt that, when necessary, GroupOne could translate his prosaic approach into a diagram that described the relationship between sales and marketing in a B2B business model.

Wallace spent another hour or so detailing the process steps and the overall value that GroupOne would offer AT. When he finally left the office, it was 9:00 P.M. Driving home, Wallace reflected on the quality of GroupOne's client relationships. Like all of GroupOne's RFP responses, their response to AT's RFP was a collaborative effort—an effort made possible by the insight and experience of GroupOne's employees.

Key Takeaways from Chapter 7

As Molly's approach to working with her accounting client and Exhibit 7-2 illustrate, it is imperative that the disciplines of sales and marketing work together in an integrated fashion through every step of the sales and marketing process, including the ongoing nurturing of the customer relationship.

In the early stages of market opportunity assessment, the nature of the work tends to be marketing centered and highly strategic. But that doesn't mean that the sales organization isn't involved. As the process moves forward, steps become more tactical in nature as the process becomes increasingly focused on execution. No matter how good an organization's strategy may be, at the end of the day, its success is predicated on how well it is executed. Failure to effectively execute a well-conceived strategy is as bad as having an ill-conceived strategy in the first place.

Exhibit 7-2

Based on Exhibit 7-2, we learn the following about developing and then executing a sales and marketing strategy:

1. **Market Assessment**—Begin with a sound strategy and a thorough, accurate assessment of the market. The marketing team takes the lead, but the sales team provides input to validate the marketplace assessment.
2. **Brand Development & Awareness**—Marketing takes the lead to develop the unique brand message and communicates the message to the marketplace. The sales team works to take the message to the street.
3. **Lead Qualification, Generation & Nurturing**—Sales and marketing share equally in the lead qualification, generation and nurturing process. Establishing the two-way dialogue with the prospect universe rests largely with the marketing team, but sales must work hand-in-hand to help define the dimensions of a qualified lead.
4. **Opportunity Development**—Once the sales organization receives a qualified lead, it is up to sales to effectively uncover the needs of the prospect that will be satisfied by the product/service. Marketing plays a supportive role in this effort.
5. **Sales Closure**—The sales team is responsible for making and closing the sale. Marketing provides support in terms of messaging and communications.
6. **Customer Relationship Development**—Sales will always take the lead in nurturing customer relationships. It is the communications between the customer and the sales person that uncovers opportunities for both cross-selling and upselling.

8
The Sales and Marketing Alignment Process

At 7:00 A.M. on Friday morning, Wallace resumed his preparation of GroupOne's response for AT's RFP. He began by reviewing his notes and contemplating how he would describe GroupOne's sales and marketing alignment model. The model, he believed, would be invaluable in showing precisely how sales and marketing should align to accomplish AT's sales objectives for SecureSoft.

As Wallace reviewed the contents of the nearly finished response, he felt that it made all the necessary points but that it lacked a cohesive framework. Nonetheless, he was confident that, by the alignment of sales and marketing, he could portray GroupOne's unique, systemic approach to sales and marketing. Wallace started reconstructing the response, beginning with a brief introduction of GroupOne's experience and business philosophy. Next, he composed a restatement of business objectives for SecureSoft, which he followed with a diagram of the sales and marketing alignment process. In describing the diagram, Wallace emphasized how it portrayed a framework of GroupOne's strategic and tactical recommendations. He began with the first step in the process, defining marketplace opportunity.

Define Marketplace Opportunity

Working hand-in-hand with AT's senior management and sales and marketing staff, GroupOne proposed an audit of available marketplace data, which they would use to create a proposal that addressed data gaps. SecureSoft lacked a sales history, and conducting this primary research would put AT in a great position to define Secure-Soft's market opportunity.

To define SecureSoft's market opportunity, Wallace knew that AT needed a clear depiction of sales revenue sources based on industry vertical and company size (firmographics). Based on the information provided in AT's RFP and their responses to the agencies' questions, this information was nonexistent. After recommending the primary research needed to gather the information, Wallace moved on to step two.

Brand Positioning and Awareness

In order to define SecureSoft's brand position, AT needed to embrace qualitative and quantitative market research. AT had defined SecureSoft's brand position solely on the opinions of its prospective customers, which was valuable information. However, to be successful in the marketplace, SecureSoft needed to base its brand position and unique value proposition on more than a company executive's "gut feeling."

Knowing that step one of the sales and marketing alignment process would offer considerable insight for the development of brand positioning, Wallace outlined a 30,000-foot view that showed how GroupOne would generate marketplace awareness for SecureSoft, articulating strategies and tactics that combined traditional print advertising, trade show demonstrations, direct mail, email, telemarketing, and web communication. After reviewing his presentation of step two, Wallace moved on to step three.

Demand Generation and Prospect Nurturing

Demand generation and prospect nurturing consists of marketing strategy supported by tactical touch points that utilize multiple forms of media to inform a product or service's prospect universe and stimulate interest in the offering. The process entails a detailed contact strategy that incorporates timing, frequency and means of contact (e.g., direct mail, email, telemarketing, webinar, etc.). In their response to AT's RFP, GroupOne incorporated the following flow chart to provide AT with a diagrammatic view of how a fully integrated, multistage demand generation program (Exhibit 8-1) would operate.

GroupOne's proposal encouraged AT to view a demand-generation solution as a long-term investment that would support both SecureSoft and AT's future products. Over the years, GroupOne had perfected the necessary factors for designing and executing effective demand generation and nurturing programs. Drawing on his experience, Wallace pointed out that the first step towards demand generation was recognizing that not every prospective customer is ready to buy when the seller is trying to sell, which means that a demand generation solution must contain a subprocess that constantly nurtures prospective customers, whether by newsletters via email, direct mail, or periodically checking in with prospective customers by telephone.

Additionally, the selling company must present their information in a timely, relevant manner. Contacting prospects too often or presenting too much information at the wrong time in the buying process can make a prospect feel pressured and overwhelmed. Periodic communication is analogous to watering a plant. The appropriate amount of contact, like the appropriate of water, nourishes growth, while too

Exhibit 8-1. Multi-Stage Integrated Demand Generation Campaign Flow

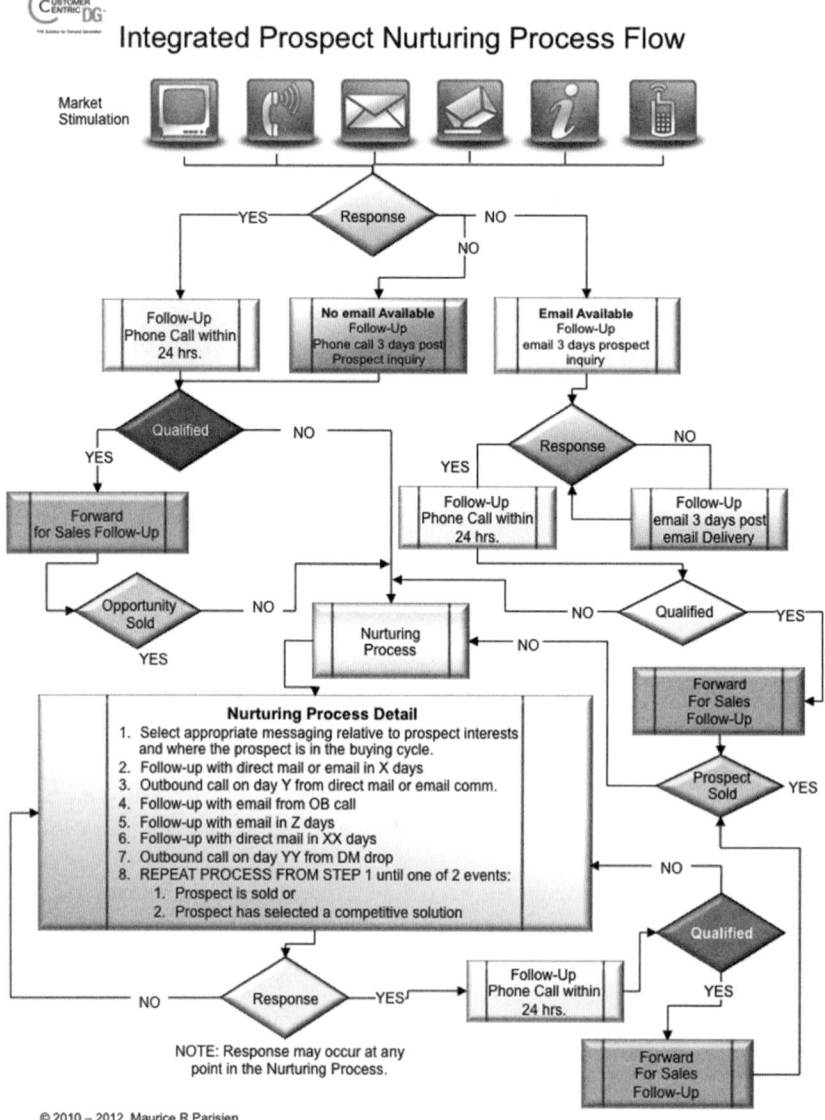

much contact, like too much water, kills growth. Ultimately, a successful demand generation program establishes a meaningful dialogue between buyer and seller, so that when the buyer has a problem that the seller can solve, a business rapport is already in place, giving the seller an advantage over competitors.

Another key factor in nurturing prospective customers is using the right kind of communication. Effective communication has three characteristics: It uses the "right" media, delivers the message at the "right" time, and makes sure that the message has

Exhibit 8-2

	Company A	Company B
Retention Rate	95%	95%
Annual Growth in Customer Acquistion	25%	10%
Customer Count At the Start	20	20
Customer Count at the End of Yr 1	24	21
Yr 2	28	22
Yr 3	33	23
Yr 4	40	24
Yr 5	47	25
Total Customer Count	47	25
Net Customer Gain	22	89.5%

the "right" content. By tracking the media consumption habits of their clients' prospective customers, GroupOne developed nurturing programs that *worked*. GroupOne assessed media habits in one of two ways: by monitoring how prospective customers received outside communication, or if the customers seemed to have no preference, by referring to the general preferences of the prospect universe.

As Wallace was completing the response, he emphasized an additional value associated with a long-term commitment to a demand generation solution: a steady stream of new customers. Although some executives like to believe that a customer will be a customer forever, customer defection is common. Even at a modest level of 5-percent defection (95 percent retention) per year, companies can still benefit by implementing an effective demand generation program. To illustrate the point of customer defection countered by an aggressive customer acquisition strategy, Wallace constructed the table in Exhibit 8-2.

Fueling Growth with Demand Generation

Exhibit 8-2 illustrates the value of retaining customers at a higher rate while fueling growth through demand generation. It assumed that both companies are able to retain 95percent of their customer base year after year for five years. However, Company A puts in place a more aggressive demand generation program that generates a compounded annual growth rate of 25 percent, while Company B achieves 10percent annual growth in customer acquisition. In the end, Company A surpasses Company B in total customers at the end of five years by a margin of 89.5percent.

To further illustrate the point, Wallace used the chart below to assign a dollar value to an aggressive versus a modest customer acquisition goal. He set the average annual dollar revenue per customer for both companies at $36,000 and then applied a future dollars discount rate of 15percent per year to calculate the net present value (NPV) of future revenues.

Exhibit 8-3

	Company A	Company B	Discount Rate	Company A (NPV Revenues)	Company B (NPV Revenues)	Variance ($)	% Var.
Retention Rate	95%	95%					
Annual Growth in Customer Acquistion	25%	10%					
Average Revenue Derived per Customer	$36,000	$36,000					
Annual Revenues at the Start	$ 720,000	720,000	1.00	$ 720,000	$ 720,000	$ -	0.0%
Total Revenues at the End of Yr 1	$ 855,000	752,400	1.15	$ 743,478	$ 654,261	$ 89,217	13.6%
Yr 2	$ 1,015,313	786,258	1.32	$ 767,722	$ 594,524	$ 173,198	29.1%
Yr 3	$ 1,205,684	821,640	1.52	$ 792,757	$ 540,241	$ 252,515	46.7%
Yr 4	$ 1,431,749	858,613	1.75	$ 818,607	$ 490,915	$ 327,692	66.8%
Yr 5	$ 1,700,202	897,251	2.01	$ 845,301	$ 446,092	$ 399,209	89.5%
Grand Total	$ 6,927,948	$ 4,836,162		$ 4,687,865	$ 3,446,034	$ 1,241,832	36.0%

The model in Exhibit 8-3 illustrated the dramatic financial advantage realized by Company A after five years.

Based on the assumptions set forth in Exhibit 8-2 on the previous page, Exhibit 8-3 projects that Company A would realize over $1.2 million dollars in gross revenues, or 36 percent more than Company B. Wallace noted that the table did not address the risk associated with running a defection rate higher than the stated 5 percent. Nonetheless, he knew that the table would help AT realize the value of a well-designed demand generation and nurturing system.

Sales Opportunity Development

In order to realize the gains projected by a demand generation system, a sales organization must be fully engaged in the process. In his response, Wallace explained that sales and marketing must be aligned, which includes three key elements from both disciplines. First, sales must work hand-in-hand with marketing to define the prospect universe; second, sales and marketing must define the parameters that constitute a qualified lead, especially in terms of prospects' needs and goals; and, finally, sales and marketing must insure that communications elements focus on the unique value proposition, engaging the prospect in a dialogue that discusses specific needs.

How did GroupOne's approach to new business development differ from its competitors? According to Wallace, the difference was grounded in GroupOne's philosophical approach to identifying and solving business issues. Some B2B companies are in the market to "sell their products and services" with no strings attached, while companies with more foresight focus on solving business issues to heighten the legitimacy and, therefore, the sales of products. In the first scenario, sales representatives approach prospect companies hoping to communicate a product's features and benefits, while the latter scenario is more customer-focused. A customer-centered sales and marketing philosophy is grounded in the knowledge of how customers make buying decisions.

To emphasize this point, Wallace introduced a "seven-step customer buying process." In the first step of the process, many business executives are unaware of their company's greater needs. After becoming aware of the needs, the executive comes to step two, where they "recognize the presence of a particular problem, need or goal." After the need is identified, most executives begin to "search for a solution," arriving at step three. After envisioning a solution, executives begin the fourth step of "assessing their options." Next, the executive arrives at the fifth step where a "decision is made." Finally, the Customer Buying Process ends with "negotiation" (Step 6), followed by "making a purchase," or not, in step seven.

Although the Customer Buying Process seems fairly intuitive, many sales organizations fail to link the "enterprise selling process" with the "customer buying process."[1] Companies that subscribe to a customer-focused approach to sales engage prospective customers by listening to their needs and goals and then offering effective solutions.

Customer Relationship Development

After detailing the customer acquisition process, Wallace decided to communicate a unique opportunity that GroupOne would offer AT: a focus on customer retention. When it comes to customer acquisition, many companies miss the opportunity to focus on initiatives that aid in the retention, growth, and advocacy of a customer base.

Retention

Working hand-in-hand, sales and marketing can insulate customers against external influences that can lead to customer defection. Wallace outlined specific strategies for retention, the first of which suggested a combination of communications, training, and education programs that would ensure that customers were maximizing SercureSoft's capabilities. As a part of this recommendation, GroupOne proposed the initiation of a SecureSoft blog and user group, which would accomplish two things: The blog would keep AT current on application issues faced by SecureSoft users and, ultimately, establish a SecureSoft "community" that would share ideas.

Next, GroupOne recommended that SecureSoft's customers be encouraged to participate in a quarterly online survey that would show AT which of SecureSoft's features/attributes customers valued most. Also, the survey would assess how well SecureSoft was living up to its predictions. If weaknesses were identified, AT could immediately correct the problem and tell users of the correction. The results of customer satisfaction research would be summarized and shared with management, software engineers, and developers, along with a list of "top priorities" to be addressed within six months. Moreover, the constant interchange of information with customers would allow AT to minimize customer defection.

Growth

The next step in the evolution of customer relationships is customer growth. In AT's case, there would likely be future opportunities to improve SecureSoft's functionality. Because SecureSoft was delivered as a SaaS solution, AT could easily

---

[1] Refer to Exhibit 3-1.

offer necessary plug-ins identified through customer satisfaction surveys or other means of dialogue. Research indicates that customer growth reduces customer defection. By keeping a close eye on the marketplace while nurturing close relationship with its customers, sales organizations stay abreast of their customers' new needs, which are often the needs of potential customers. GroupOne had worked with a number of clients and found that, for every step in the customer relationship process, a close relationship between sales and marketing disciplines was critical to the expansion of customer relationships.

Advocacy

The last step in the customer relationship process is advocacy. A SecureSoft blog would lead to advocacy for SecureSoft. GroupOne had learned that, once customers are satisfied with a product or service, they are usually willing to lend their support in the form recommendations. If GroupOne won AT's business, GroupOne would plan, design, and execute an advocacy program for SecureSoft, aligning sales and marketing in the process.

Steps for Sales and Marketing Alignment

Wallace thought that it would be helpful to outline the steps that would lead to the alignment of AT's sales and marketing disciplines. Whether or not AT outsourced sales and/or marketing functions, GroupOne believed that it would be imperative for AT's sales and marketing disciplines to operate in alignment. Like most changes that management wants to bring about in an organization, the alignment of the sales and marketing process is expressed in a few basic steps:

- Planning and Process Design
- Execution
- Measurement
- Refinement

Planning and Process Design

In the first step towards alignment, GroupOne proposed to assist AT with assessing AT's current sales and marketing disciplines. Based on the replies to the questions posed to Joe Albright, Wallace was aware that AT was currently searching for a senior sales executive, which presented a perfect opportunity to create a comprehensive sales development process.

Wallace recalled that AT lacked formalized marketing programs. Thus, like the sales process, the marketing process would be created from scratch. To provide AT with an idea of the elements that would comprise an aligned sales and marketing process, Wallace inserted a one-page chart that offered a broad view of the combined processes.[2]

---

[2] See appendix page ii for a full description of the Sales & Marketing Alignment Continuum

In addition, GroupOne proposed assisting AT in defining the individual roles and responsibilities associated with each of the process elements outlined in the sales and marketing alignment continuum. Having performed this service for a number of other clients, GroupOne believed that AT would perceive this service as a "value-add."

Execution

The next step in creating sales and marketing alignment was to work with AT and its newly hired sales executive to implement well-defined process elements. Implementation of the various sales and marketing processes would be accomplished over a 90-day period, becoming fully operational in four months. Any systems requirements (e.g., sales automation or CRM solutions) would require additional time and would likely follow a period of manual process implementation that refined the various processes and sub-processes.

Measurement

Key metrics and key performance indicators (KPI) would be identified early in the process to focus AT's attention on predicting market performance. In a demand-generation program, the focus would be on such things as the number of qualified leads delivered to a sales team on a weekly/monthly basis, the number of closed sales, average revenue per sale, gross profit per sale, and monthly return on marketing investment calculated on a cumulative basis. But before this could happen, AT's senior management, finance department and sales and marketing departments needed to agree on what metrics should be used.

Refinement

During the first 90 days of a new sales and marketing process, there typically are opportunities for improvement. GroupOne would propose a monthly review of program performance in the form of "monthly quality process improvement sessions," during which opportunities for improvement would be documented. Although the work level for implementing AT's new sales and marketing processes would not warrant a Six Sigma initiative, Wallace thought it made good sense to apply the Six Sigma DMAIC process steps as a framework to *define, measure, analyze, improve* and *control* the process on an ongoing basis. He decided to incorporate a simple DMAIC map to illustrate the steps of the process and the components of the steps. The diagram in Exhibit 8-4 illustrates the Six Sigma DMAIC process.[3]

It was late on Friday afternoon and Wallace was putting the finishing touches on GroupOne's response to AT's RFP. He had just completed the time line and a preliminary line item budget when Brian Walker stopped by to see how he was doing.

"Wallace, how's it going?"

---

[3] Pyzdek, Thomas (2003) *The Six Sigma Handbook—Revised and Expanded Edition,* New York, McGraw-Hill

Exhibit 8-4. Six Sigma Diagram

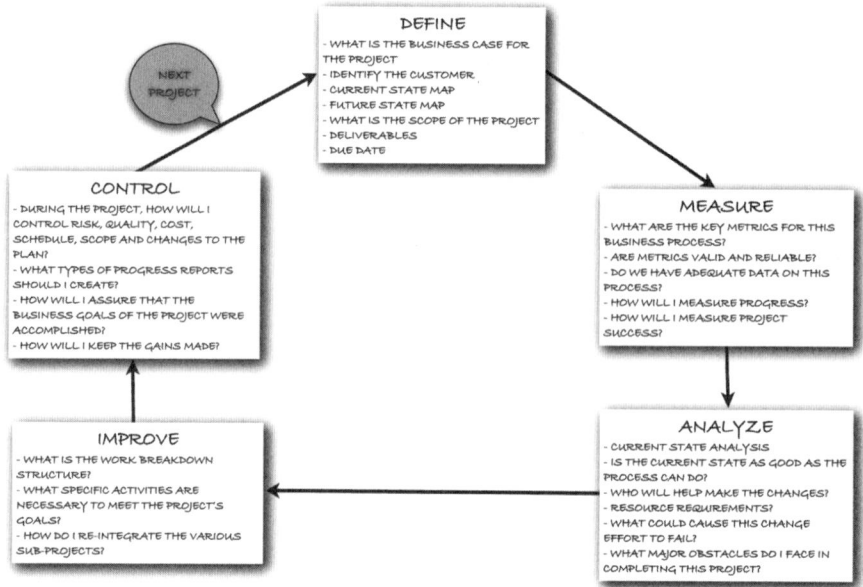

"Fine, Brian. I've almost completed a draft of the AT response."

"That's great, Wallace. Thanks for meeting the deadline."

"Not a problem, Brian. This is an exciting opportunity for us and I hope we win it. I'm just applying some finishing touches. I'll get this off to you and the others before I leave tonight. Assuming we get input from the other team members by close of business on Monday, we'll be in great shape to get this to Joe Albright on Tuesday and beat our deadline."

"Again, Wallace, great job. I'll look forward to reviewing the proposal. Have a great weekend."

"Thanks, Brian. You do the same."

Wallace did a final review of the RFP response. He found a number of grammatical and punctuation errors, but he was mainly challenging himself to think through the framework of the response by thinking through some basic and fundamental questions:

- Is the response easy to follow?
- Is it well thought through?
- Does the response address all of the questions posed in the RFP?
- If AT accepts and implements this proposal, will it achieve the stated business goals for SecureSoft?
- Does the framework tie together the flow of the response?

Key Takeaways from Chapter 8

After a business acquires customers, it's important that it realize the economic value of retaining and growing customer relationships. When contemplating the value of customer relationships, managers should take the time to quantify the value of customer relationships by working through a process of profiling and segmentation. Understanding that no two customers are alike, it is important to quantify the value of each customer segment in terms of the current value derived from the relationship, as well as the potential value of the relationship based on current "share-of-wallet" and value to be derived downstream through the customer development process.

Additionally, employing the Six Sigma process to sales and marketing delivers a disciplined and repeatable approach to continuously improving business performance. For years, the Six Sigma process has been a widely deployed for the manufacturing process. But only within the past few years has it been implemented within the sales and marketing process. In the Appendix of this book are numerous references to Six Sigma and the steps that one can take to design an effective framework for implementing the Six Sigma process to strengthen and improve the effectiveness of the sales and marketing process.

- Is the case made for implementing a multistage, multi-media demand generation program?
- Based on the financials provided by AT, do the sales and marketing recommendations make financial sense?
- Assuming that the plan delivers the anticipated results, is the Return on Marketing Investment (ROMI) attractive enough in all cases (best, probable, worst)?
- Does GroupOne's Unique Value Proposition (UVP) come through in the response?
- Given the choice of four agencies, has the case been made for AT to select GroupOne over the other 3 agencies?

After completing his review, Wallace attached the response to an email with a brief message to the team members and Paul Austin. He clicked the 'Send' button, shut down his computer, slipped the RFP response into his brief case and turned out the lights. It was time to let the weekend get underway.

9
Narrowing the Field

On Thursday morning, Joe Albright began reviewing the RFP responses. He forwarded them to Frank and Marlie so they could do the same. Based on the original time line that Joe and the Scotts had put together two weeks ago, they were on track to select the agency two days ahead of schedule. They planned on narrowing the list of candidates to two within the next three days, which would give the finalists roughly two weeks to prepare formal presentations for AT's review.

Joe decided to plan a meeting with Frank and Marlie to review their assessment of the agency responses. An hour after he had sent off a request to meet with the Scotts on the following Monday, they responded that meeting at 1:30 P.M. would work best.

In reviewing the RFP responses, Joe began with Slone Direct. Slone's response was fairly light in content. The response did not focus much attention on strategies that addressed AT's marketing challenges. Instead, their response concentrated on tactical concepts. They offered some interesting ideas towards integrating communications, such as using direct mail and email to generate interest in SecureSoft among mid-tier companies, but they did not propose split testing, which Joe found surprising.

Nonetheless, Slone did have several strong points. For one, they had been around for 10 years. When Joe ran a D&B report on Slone, he found that the company was financially stable and had a good track record of paying their suppliers according to terms. Joe was also impressed with the caliber of the team that Slone had assembled to work with AT. In addition, upon reviewing the case studies in Slone's response, he saw examples of successful marketing campaigns in terms of response and conversion data. Yet, the case studies failed to reveal hard financial data, making it impossible to calculate ROI. Upon completing his review, Joe opened a blank scorecard from his computer's desktop and began inserting numbers, calculating them according to the categorical weightings to arrive at Slone's total score.

Exhibit 9-1. Slone Direct's Scorecard

Criteria	Weighting	Score (1-5 w/ 5=outstanding)	Total
1. Industry experience	7	4	28
2. Agency size	6	3	18
3. Agency years in business	5	5	25
4. Proposal cost vs. services delivered	8	3	24
5. Financial stability	8	4	32
6. Percent client retention	8	3	16
7. Senior management commitment	11	4	44
8. Caliber of the team assigned to the business	12	4	48
9. Caliber of references of existing and prior clients	15	TBD	0
10. Demonstrated expertise in managing fully integrated marketing mix elements e.g., print, direct mail, telemarketing, email, web (SEO, PPC, Internet marketing)	20	3	60
Total	100		295

Slone's total score of 295 was mediocre at best, but Joe still needed to obtain references from the agency's clients. However, even a perfect score in this area would not result in a great overall score. Slone's two lowest scores came in "proposal cost vs. services delivered" and "client retention." Their response to proposal cost seemed evasive, and several elements in their tactical plan were undeveloped, leaving Joe to guess about their cost. He would have rather seen Slone make general assumptions instead of leaving this critical point unaddressed. Concerning client retention, AT's RFP asked each agency to list clients that represented 80 percent of the agency's billings for the current year, submit a client list for the two previous years containing the total billings for each client and indicate the month and year a client was acquired. This data showed that, in the last two years, Slone had retained only 30 percent of clients that comprised the lower third of its top accounts. After finishing Slone's scorecard, Joe moved on to The Foster Group.

Exhibit 9-2. The Foster Group's Scorecard

Criteria	Weighting	Score (1-5 w/ 5=outstanding)	Total
1. Industry experience	7	5	35
2. Agency size	6	4	24
3. Agency years in business	5	5	25
4. Proposal cost vs. services delivered	8	2	16
5. Financial stability	8	4	32
6. Percent client retention	8	3	24
7. Senior management commitment	11	4	44
8. Caliber of the team assigned to the business	12	4	48
9. Caliber of references of existing and prior clients	15	TBD	0
10. Demonstrated expertise in managing fully integrated marketing mix elements e.g., print, direct mail, telemarketing, email, web (SEO, PPC, Internet marketing)	20	3	60
Total	100		308

The Foster Group scored better than Slone Direct, but a score of 308 was still marginal. As with Slone, Joe had not contacted The Foster Group's references, but, again, a high rating in this area could not compensate for the marginal ratings in other areas.

Next, Joe evaluated MarCom Solutions. Based on his conference call with MarCom, Joe was impressed with their commitment to success, but he was careful not to let first impressions influence final evaluations.

Exhibit 9-3. MarCom Solutions' Scorecard

Criteria	Weighting	Score (1-5 w/ 5=outstanding)	Total
1. Industry experience	7	5	35
2. Agency size	6	4	24
3. Agency years in business	5	4	20
4. Proposal cost vs. services delivered	8	4	32
5. Financial stability	8	4	32
6. Percent client retention	8	4	32
7. Senior management commitment	11	4	44
8. Caliber of the team assigned to the business	12	3	36
9. Caliber of references of existing and prior clients	15	TBD	0
10. Demonstrated expertise in managing fully integrated marketing mix elements e.g., print, direct mail, telemarketing, email, web (SEO, PPC, Internet marketing)	20	3	60
Total	100		315

Based on raw score, MarCom would be one of the two final candidates. Again, Joe needed to check references, but he felt that this criterion would be most helpful in separating the two final agencies. The weakest criterion in MarCom's evaluation was the lack of experience of its team that would be helping AT. This factor weighed heavy in Joe's mind as he considered his final recommendation to the Scotts.

Finally, Joe began evaluating GroupOne, which had obviously invested a great deal of time and energy in presenting a response with great face quality. Each of the response's sections neatly outlined each element in AT's RFP. In addition to great style, the response also had substance. The content concerning the customer buying process and the alignment of sales and marketing was well presented, but most impressive of all were the biographies of GroupOne's team members that would be working with AT. After spending an hour reviewing GroupOne's response, Joe completed the scorecard.

Exhibit 9-4. GroupOne's Scorecard

Criteria	Weighting	Score (1-5 w/ 5=outstanding)	Total
1. Industry experience	7	5	35
2. Agency size	6	3	18
3. Agency years in business	5	3	15
4. Proposal cost vs. services delivered	8	5	40
5. Financial stability	8	5	40
6. Percent client retention	8	5	40
7. Senior management commitment	11	5	55
8. Caliber of the team assigned to the business	12	5	60
9. Caliber of references of existing and prior clients	15	TBD	0
10. Demonstrated expertise in managing fully integrated marketing mix elements e.g., print, direct mail, telemarketing, email, web (SEO, PPC, Internet marketing)	20	5	100
Total	100		403

Joe was not surprised that GroupOne's score was 28 percent higher than the previous high score set by MarCom. GroupOne's two lowest scores were in agency size and years in business. These criteria were important, but their weightings were the lowest. Joe knew that an agency's size should take a back seat to its ability to perform. After all, if AT went with a larger agency, there was a good chance that marketing efforts for AT would take a back seat to programs managed for larger clients.

Joe called Frank to see if he had started reviewing the responses. "Hi, Frank, it's Joe Albright. How's it going this afternoon?"

"It's going well, Joe. We're making progress with candidates for our sales executive role."

"That's great to hear. How did you find the candidates?" Joe asked.

"Remember me telling you that I was going to do some networking with some of our business associates?"

"Sure," Joe replied.

"Well, an old friend of mine gave me the names of few sales executives that are currently employed but might be interested in talking. I had coffee with one of them on Tuesday and we agreed to have a follow-up meeting in another week. This guy has the experience we're looking for and he has a solid track record of B2B sales."

"Sounds promising, Frank."

"I hope it is. The sooner we get someone hired the better. So, what's up on your side of the fence?"

"Well, the reason I called was to see if you and Marlie had started reviewing the agency responses."

"I don't know about Marlie," Frank replied, "but I haven't spent much time on them. Are we still on for our review meeting next Monday?"

"Yes, we are. I've just spent most of today reviewing the responses, including completing the scorecards, and thought I'd check to see if you and Marlie had done the same."

"We haven't, but we soon will. We'll be taking the responses home tonight, but we probably won't have them completed until the weekend."

"Oh, that's fine, Frank. I just thought I'd check-in. I did forward you the hard copies that we received from the agencies, right?"

"Yes, you did," Frank replied, "and, I have to tell you, I'm initially impressed by GroupOne."

"I had the same reaction," Joe replied, "and I think you'll be even more impressed with the substance of their response. On the subject of recruiting a sales executive, I wanted to let you know that I'd be happy to assist in the interviewing process.

"That would be helpful, Joe. I'd appreciate your involvement."

"Then count me in," Joe responded. "You could insert me into the process following your next interview with the current candidate. We can talk following your next meeting and discuss the strengths that the executive should have. Have you thought about putting these candidates through a formal selection assessment process?"

"I've given it some thought, but I don't know of any local firms that provide that service. Do you know of any?"

"Yes, I do. A year ago, I worked with a company that specialized in the selection and hiring process for mid- to upper-level business executives across all disciplines. I'll give them a call and see if they can help."

"That would be a big help," sighed Frank.

"One more thing, Frank. We'll definitely need to check the references provided by the sales executive candidates and, when we reach that point, I'll help you do it."

"That would be a big help as well. Let's see how my next meeting goes with the current candidate. If all goes well, I think it would be good to engage a management/HR consulting firm to put the candidate through a series of assessments and, at the same time, we could be following up with his references."

"Sounds good, Frank. Just let me know when I can help. I'll also get back to you with the name of the consulting firm that I'm thinking about. If I don't talk to you before our meeting on Monday, have a great weekend."

"You do the same, Joe. Thanks for calling."

Frank and Marlie were addressing some issues with SecureSoft, working out some bugs and coming up with some updates. Frank turned to Marlie. "Honey, that was Joe on the phone. He was checking to see if we had reviewed the agency responses. I told him that we hadn't, but that we'd start on it this evening and finish over the weekend."

"Has Joe started on the responses?" Marlie asked.

"Yes, he has. In fact, he's already completed scorecards," Frank replied.

"Wow, no moss under his feet," replied Marlie. Frank smiled. "Honey," Marlie continued, "why don't we go to Starbucks on Saturday morning and work on the responses until we get them done. We'll find a quiet corner, hunker down, and get through the responses by noon."

"That's sounds like a great idea," Frank replied.

It was a sunny autumn Saturday morning of 65 degrees. It had been two weeks since Frank and Marlie had taken their Harley out for a ride.

"Hey, why don't we take the Harley over to Starbucks?" Frank beamed.

"That sounds like fun," Marlie replied. "I'll grab our helmets."

The Scotts grabbed the agency responses and their laptops, placed them in the bike's saddlebags, and off they went. At Starbucks, they found a quiet corner and settled into its overstuffed chairs.

"What can I get you," asked Frank to Marlie?

"I'll take a grandé coffee and a blueberry muffin. Thanks."

With breakfast in hand, the Scotts started reviewing the responses. They decided to review each response simultaneously in case one of them had a question that the other could answer. They began with The Foster Group, whose proposal was a brief nine pages.

They felt that the response lacked strategic depth and failed to offer what they wanted in integrated marketing communications. Without checking The Foster Group's client references, Frank and Marlie arrived at raw scores of 295 and 288, respectively. Like Joe, they felt that client references could be postponed until evaluating the two final agencies.

The Scotts moved on to Slone Direct. At eight pages, Slone's response was briefer than The Foster Group's and showed even less strategic insight. AT's RFP had stressed the importance of sales and marketing initiatives in achieving its business goals. The Scotts were disappointed to see the sketchy thought given to strategic and tactical programs. Without a marketing plan that delivered the volume of qualified leads required to meet revenue targets, AT could never realize its goals. Frank and Marlie scored Slone Direct at 276 and 283, respectively.

Frank and Marlie were ready for refills on their coffee. "Marlie, do you want anything else?"

"No thanks, a refill will be fine. Ask them to leave a little more room for cream."

"Will do," Frank replied as he headed towards the counter.

When he returned, the Scotts began reviewing the response from MarCom

Solutions. It was stronger than the previous responses. While it lacked the depth of strategic thought that the Scotts wanted, it presented impressive ideas on tactical lead generation and demand generation programs. The Scotts sensed that MarCom's senior management was committed to providing the kind of marketing solutions necessary to achieve AT's business goals. One sign of this commitment came from the cover letter to MarCom's response. In it, MarCom's president, Stephen Collins, pledged that MarCom would devote senior resources to helping AT. After scoring MarCom's response, both Frank and Marlie arrived at a total score of 326.

It was 11:00 A.M. and the Scotts had one response to go. As they began reviewing GroupOne's response, they were impressed with the quality of its graphics and well-organized information. After a careful review, they were equally impressed with the response's quality of thought. The process elements of the customer buying process and the process for the alignment of the sales and marketing disciplines were both intuitive and presented with utter simplicity. The proposal's list source strategies for the development of the prospect database demonstrated a clear understanding of what AT wanted to accomplish with SecureSoft. Also impressive was the caliber of the GroupOne team that would work with AT.

After Frank gave GroupOne a score of 409 and Marlie arrived at a score of 403, they decided to jot some notes to themselves in preparation for the Monday afternoon meeting with Joe. Just before noon, Frank and Marlie packed up their belongings and left Starbucks.

On Monday morning, Joe was on his office phone with a management consultant he had worked with several years back on a management recruitment engagement. The consultant's name was Bob Williamson. Bob held a Ph.D. in industrial and organizational psychology. He had been a management consultant for more than twenty years. His area of expertise was occupational psychology and talent assessment, with particular emphasis on the disciplines of sales and marketing. Joe explained to Bob what he and AT wanted to accomplish in the selection of a highly qualified and experienced sales executive. After Joe described AT's business goals, Bob asked a few questions to make sure that he was clear on AT's business needs and that he understood AT's current management dynamics. Joe ended the conversation by telling Bob that he would call him after he spoke with Frank and Marlie.

Joe showed up at the offices of AT 15 minutes before the scheduled 1:30 meeting. He stopped by Frank and Marlie's office to let them know that he had arrived and then found his way to the conference room. Once he got to the conference room, Joe reached into his backpack and pulled out the agencies' RFP responses along with his laptop to prepare for the meeting. He then walked to the front of the conference room, grabbed some markers, and went to the whiteboard. He drew four columns for the scorecard criteria, one for each agency. Frank and Marlie arrived in the conference room promptly at 1:30.

"Hi Frank. Hi Marlie. How are the both of you?" Joe began.

"Doing well, Joe," Frank replied, "and you?"

"I couldn't be better. I'm anxious to hear your impressions and see your scorecards for the agencies. In fact, if you're both ready, let's just jump into our individual assessments for each of the agencies' responses. On the whiteboard, I've posted a summary scorecard that we can use to fill in the total score that each of us assigned to each of the agencies for each criterion. In the end, we can come up with a total of our scores for each of the agencies and an average for the three of us. Sound good?"

"Perfect, Joe," replied Marlie. Frank nodded in agreement.

"Okay, let's get started. Frank, why don't you go first and give me your scores for each of the agencies on each criterion? Let's start with the first criterion, industry expertise."

Joe walked to the whiteboard and tallied the scores for each of the evaluators, beginning with Frank. Marlie gave her responses next, and then Joe posted his scores.

Exhibit 9-5. Summary Scorecard

Criteria/Agencies	The Foster Group	Slone Direct	MarCom Solutions	GroupOne
Industry experience	28/35/35	28/21/28	35/35/35	35/35/35
Agency size	18/24/24	18/18/18	24/24/24	24/18/18
Agency years in business	25/25/25	25/25/25	20/20/20	15/15/15
Proposal cost vs. services delivered	16/16/16	24/24/24	32/32/32	40/40/40
Financial stability	32/32/32	32/32/32	32/32/32	40/40/40
Percent client retention	24/24/24	16/16/16	32/32/32	40/40/40
Senior management commitment	44/44/44	44/44/44	55/55/44	55/55/55
Caliber of the team assigned to the business	48/48/48	36/36/48	36/36/36	60/60/60
Caliber of references of existing and prior clients	0/0/0	0/0/0	0/0/0	0/0/0
Demonstrated expertise in managing fully integrated marketing mix elements	60/40/60	60/60/60	60/60/60	100/100/100
Total	295/288/308	283/276/295	326/326/315	409/403/403

Exhibit 9-6. Summary Scorecard Total Scores

The Foster Group	Slone Direct	MarCom Solutions	GroupOne
297	285	322	405

Following the tabulation of the scores, it was clear that the top two agencies were MarCom and GroupOne, but GroupOne was by far the top performer, outpacing MarCom by 83 points. Tipping the scale in GroupOne's favor was its demonstrated expertise in managing integrated marketing campaigns and the mix of communications elements associated with those campaigns.

Joe turned to Frank and Marlie for their thoughts on the scoring and agency selection process. "Marlie, do you have any particular thoughts on the evaluation process that we've gone through?"

"Well, as I reflect on the ten criteria that we selected, along with the weighting that we applied to each one, I think that we came up with a thorough and equitable approach to select the top two firms. I can't think of a better approach than the process that we just completed."

"Frank, what do you think?"

"I agree with Marlie. I think that we've come to an intelligent and fair conclusion. I'd suggest that we move forward from this point by contacting the two agencies that didn't make it to the finals and inform them of our decision. I'd also suggest that we contact the people at MarCom and GroupOne to see when we can schedule their presentations."

"I agree," replied Joe. "Given that I've been the point person on this initiative thus far, if it's okay with you two, I'll notify the agencies of our decisions."

"That would be great, Joe," Frank replied.

"We should probably give the folks at MarCom and GroupOne at least ten days to develop their presentations," Joe suggested.

"I agree," Frank replied.

"If I can shift gears for a second," Joe began, "I talked to the management consulting firm that I mentioned in our conversation last week, Frank. I spoke with a fellow by the name of Bob Williamson. He has a Ph.D. in industrial and organizational psychology and specializes in executive coaching and selection assessments for executives in sales and marketing. I told him what we were working on and he said that he would welcome the opportunity to meet with you and Marlie."

"Frank," Marlie jumped in, "I don't need to be a part of that discussion. If you'd like to meet with this consultant one on one, I'm fine with that."

"However you'd like it is fine with me," Frank responded. "Joe, why don't you give Dr. Williamson my contact information and tell him to call me about a meeting time."

"I'll do it, Frank. Is there anything else we need to discuss at this point?"

"I think we're done here," Frank replied.

"Thanks for the putting together the RFP response and this evaluation process," Marlie said. "I think it's gotten us to a point where we've definitely come down to the top two agencies."

"Thanks, Marlie. I appreciate the kind words. If you don't mind, I'd like to camp out here and make my calls to the agencies."

"Fine with me, Joe," Frank replied.

Frank left the conference room and Joe began making calls, beginning with Slone Direct. He reached the VP of Client Services, Mary McCarty, and informed her of AT's decision. The call was brief. She expressed her disappointment, but thanked Joe for the opportunity to submit their response to the RFP.

The second call went out to David Foster, the founder and president of The Foster Group. Joe was able to catch David at his desk and informed him of the decision. David expressed his disappointment and asked a few questions concerning why his agency was not selected. Joe provided him with feedback that came straight from the scorecard.

Joe's third call was to John Moloney, VP of Sales for MarCom Solutions. Joe reached John in his office and informed him that his agency had been selected to formally present their RFP response. Joe asked John for some meeting times that might work within the next two weeks. John asked if he could get back to Joe after he consulted his staff and expressed his gratitude for the opportunity to participate as a finalist.

The final call was to GroupOne's Brian Walker. Cynthia, GroupOne's receptionist, received the call and asked Joe to hold while she checked to see if Brian was at his desk. Cynthia came back on the line and then transferred the call to Brian.

"Brian, this is Joe Albright. How are you this afternoon?"

"I'm great, Joe. Good to hear from you. Have you and AT reached a decision?"

"We have, Brian, and I'm pleased to inform you that GroupOne has been selected as one of two agencies to come to AT's offices for a formal presentation. We'd like to schedule the presentation within the next two weeks. The goal of your presentation will be to present your agency's capabilities along with your plan for SecureSoft."

"Joe, I couldn't receive any better news than this on a Monday afternoon. We really appreciate the opportunity to participate as a finalist. As far as the next two weeks goes, do you have a date in mind?"

"No, we don't, Brian. We want to give you some time to prepare, but we'd like to see this process completed within the next 10 to 14 days."

"Alright. Let me talk with our team and get back to you with some dates and times. How much time will we be allotted for the presentation?"

"We'd like to keep it within 90 minutes," Joe replied. "Maybe 60 minutes for presentation and 30 for Q&A."

"Sounds great, Joe. I'll email you tomorrow with some dates and times."

"Thanks, Brian. I'll look forward to your email." Before ending the call, Brian expressed his thanks once more.

The next morning, Joe received an email from Brian suggesting three meeting times within the next seven days. Joe quickly checked with Frank and Marlie for their open dates and times. The meeting with GroupOne was set for one week from

Key Takeaways from Chapter 9

As Joe Albright demonstrated, whenever you face a decision of selecting one option over another, it is wise to first identify the key criteria that represent the distinguishing characteristics associated with the value to be derived from the ultimate selection. In Joe's case, *industry experience, agency size, years in business*, along with other criteria, help to define the distinguishing characteristics that an agency would bring to AT. After identifying key criteria, it is important to apply some form of weighting to each criterion. No two criteria are alike in terms of importance. Therefore, a form of weighting that distinguishes each criterion should be devised.

Taking the time to develop criteria weighting will aid in the decision-making process by eliminating subjectivity. When constructing a weighting matrix, it is best to consider selecting the fewest possible number of criteria that will effectively frame the dimensions of the decision. The decision matrix process is intended to aid the decision-maker by coming up with the fewest possible number of criteria—sometimes referred to as the "critical few"—instead creating a long list of criteria.

In the case of AT's agency selection process, the decision matrix provided AT's management team with an effective tool that objectively narrowed the field of agency choices in a fair, unbiased and objective manner.

Tuesday at 2:00 P.M. Joe then fired off an email to John Moloney at MarCom Solutions suggesting a 9:00 A.M. meeting on the same day. John responded within the hour, indicating that the date and time would work fine. The stage was set for the finalists.

10
MarCom Solutions versus GroupOne

Early the next day, Joe was at his desk composing an outline of presentation expectations to send to GroupOne and MarCom Solutions. The agencies had one week to prepare their presentations. They would have 90 minutes of presentation time, including time for questions and answers. Joe outlined what he thought would be the best approach for gaining a full understanding of each agency's qualities and capabilities. As he recorded his notes on a legal pad, they took the following form.

  I. Agency Background
     A. Vision, mission, values
     B. Introduction to the principals
     C. Agency size, industry experience, number of clients, and share of agency revenues
     D. Awards and recognition
 II. AT/SecureSoft Marketing Plan Recommendations
III. Budget
 IV. Time line
  V. Case studies
 VI. Why select this agency?
VII. Any other element that the agency believes relevant to evaluating its bid for the business.
VIII. Q&A

After a few minor edits to the outline, Joe prepared a Word document and attached it to an email to Frank and Marlie. After sending the email, Joe called Bob Williamson to pass along the details of his conversation with Frank about involving Bob in the sales executive selection process:

"Hi, Bob. It's Joe Albright. Do you have a few minutes?"

"Sure, Joe. What's up?"

"I spoke with Frank Scott, the co-founder of AT, and he would like to meet with you to learn about the selection process you use."

"When ?"

"The meeting needs to happen as soon as possible," Joe replied. "Frank has already interviewed one candidate and has a follow-up interview planned for this week."

"That's fine. If you give me Frank's contact information, I can call him today."

"I'm in the process of sending you an email with his information as we speak. I'll copy Frank on my message so he'll know to expect your call."

"Sounds good, Joe. Thanks for thinking of me. Your email just arrived."

"Great. Take care, Bob. We'll be talking soon."

Joe checked his email and saw that Frank and Marlie had responded with some comments about the outline. Their message contained just three words: "Go for it."

Joe began composing email messages to both agencies. He addressed the messages to John Moloney and Brian Walker. Within an hour, Brian and John replied that they had received the outline. Brian asked if he could contact Joe if GroupOne had any questions as they prepared for their presentation, to which Joe happily agreed.

Following his receipt of Joe's email, John emailed Robert Hunte, his senior account person assigned to the AT opportunity, to request a meeting to discuss the presentation. Robert quickly responded, suggesting that they include Christine Marquette. John agreed on including Christine and sent out a meeting request. To keep MarCom's president, Stephen Collins, in the loop, he decided to copy him on the email. The meeting was set for the following morning.

The next morning, John Moloney arrived at the conference room at 8:50 to organize his thoughts for the meeting. Christine arrived at the top of the hour, followed by Robert just a few minutes later. Stephen stopped in to see how things were going.

"Thanks for copying me on the meeting request, John. I just thought I'd stop by to see how our opportunity with Advanced Technologies is progressing. I see that the formal presentation is on Tuesday of next week. Were you counting on me to attend?"

"I leave that up to you. I don't think it's absolutely necessary, but it would be helpful if you could."

"Unfortunately," Stephen replied, "I'll be with another client on Tuesday."

"Well, I think we'll be OK," said John. "We haven't gotten to the point of who will be attending, but I think that Robert, Christine, and myself is what we'll end up with."

"Sounds good, John. I'm sure the three of you will do fine."

"Thanks, Stephen," John replied. "We're counting on it."

After Stephen left the conference room, John, Christine, and Robert studied the presentation outline provided by Joe Albright and then reviewed their response to

AT's RFP. John suggested that they share in the delivery of the presentation. He felt that it would be best if he delivered the material on MarCom's background and experience and that Robert should present the plan recommendations. Christine would comment on the plan recommendations and present selected case studies. Robert volunteered to create the PowerPoint presentation and Christine planned to arrange the leave behind materials, which would include MarCom's company history, the RFP response and case studies. John would deliver the closing comments concerning why MarCom would be the best choice for AT. Wrapping up the meeting, John asked Robert if he had any ideas that would strengthen the presentation.

"I do," said Robert. "How about bringing in some samples of our direct mail pieces that we've created for some of our B2B clients."

"Good idea, Robert." John replied. "Maybe we can use samples that tie directly to the case studies. Can we make that happen, Christine?"

"I believe so. I'll look in the files and see what we have for samples."

"Can anyone think of anything else?" John asked.

"No, I think that does it, John," Robert replied. "In the next day or so I'll create the PowerPoint presentation and send it to you and Christine by Thursday afternoon. That should give us plenty of time to make revisions before the presentation on Tuesday."

"One more thing," John said. "I think it would be a good idea to do a practice run on Monday to ensure that we've got our ducks in a row." Christine and Robert agreed. "Thanks to the both of you for helping with this presentation. I'm confident that we'll be putting our best foot forward."

There was considerable excitement brewing at the offices of GroupOne. After receiving Joe's call, Brian sent a companywide email informing everyone that GroupOne was in the final running for the AT opportunity. With one week to go before the presentation, Brian called a meeting between the presentation's participants: Paul Austin, Susan Chapman, Stephanie Atwood, Wallace Jones, and himself. He requested to meet at 9:00 A.M. the following morning. Within an hour, everyone had responded that they could make the meeting. Brian then forwarded the attendees Joe's outline, asking them to review it and prepare responses.

The next morning, Brian's team gathered in GroupOne's main conference room. Brian kicked off the meeting by thanking everyone for his or her participation. Then he did something a little unusual. He asked Wallace to come to the front of the room. "Just so each of you will know why we're here today to discuss this opportunity, I want to introduce you to the gentleman who's responsible for it. Wallace, on behalf of the agency and your fellow employees, I want to thank you for doing an outstanding job of preparing the response to AT's RFP. After reviewing your work for a third time last night, it was clear to me why we made it to the finals. You captured the essence of GroupOne's philosophy and value proposition, and you prepared a business appeal that will be tough for a competing agency to top. Thanks for a job well done."

The room burst into applause. Wallace graciously accepted the praise and returned to his seat. Brian turned to the conference table and commended the others for their commitment to excellence. Then he asked Paul Austin to say a few words about the AT opportunity.

"I'd like to start by congratulating the entire team for getting us this far," said Paul. He grabbed the RFP response from the conference table and lifted it high in the air. "This is a quality piece of work and should become a gold standard that future agency presentations are modeled after."

Paul placed the response back on the table and turned to Brian. "Brian, you're spearheading this opportunity, but I want you to know that I'd welcome the opportunity to participate in the presentation and play whatever role you'd like me to play."

"Thanks for your support, Paul. We welcome your participation in whatever way you'd like to offer it." Brian opened his laptop and turned on the LED projector, opening a file that outlined the specific requirements for the presentation. "Before we get started, does anyone have any thoughts regarding the flow of the presentation as set forth in the outline?" Susan Chapman raised her hand. "Yes, Susan."

"Just one thing at the outset, Brian. I noted that the client indicated that they wanted to see some case studies. Since the account services team had been spending considerable time preparing a format for our case studies, I'd like the opportunity to deliver or share in the delivery of this portion of the presentation."

"Thanks for volunteering, Susan. When we get to that point in our discussion, we'll make a final decision on presenting the case studies."

Brian began the discussion by suggesting that Paul take the lead in presenting GroupOne's vision, mission, values, background, and unique value proposition. Next, he suggested that Wallace present the official plan, budget proposal, and suggested time line. Susan's interest in presenting the case studies made good sense, so she would be doing that. Finally, Brian would wrap up the formal presentation with the rationale for selecting GroupOne over the competing agency. As a special addition to the presentation, Brian asked Stephanie to create a PowerPoint presentation that articulated what a multistaged, integrated demand-generation program would look like. After an hour of fruitful discussion, Brian adjourned the meeting by suggesting that the team reconvene on Friday afternoon for a brief progress report.

The next two days passed quickly. Brian assembled the team in the conference room to check on the progress of the presentation. "Well team, how are we doing? Susan, let's start with you. What kind of progress have you made with the PowerPoint presentation?"

"It's almost finished, Brian. I'm also working closely with Stephanie to strengthen the appeal for the demand generation program. We've added another dimension that incorporates a comprehensive process map that links to the tactical elements of direct mail, email, telemarketing, print advertising, and web pages."

"Very cool, Susan," Brian responded. "I can't wait to see how all of this comes together. Does anyone else have an update for us?"

"I'm working with our production people to assemble hard copies of our response and the integrated, multistage demand-generation plan that we proposed," said Wallace.

"Great, Wallace. Anyone else?" No one spoke up, so Brian moved on. "It sounds like we have a lot going on and that we're all moving down the right path. Let's touch base one more time on Monday afternoon to run through our presentation and see if any last-minute details need to be addressed." With that, the meeting adjourned and everyone returned to working on their presentation elements.

The weekend came and went. The MarCom team gathered to review their PowerPoint presentation along with sample materials that were prepared for Tuesday's presentation. John Moloney led the meeting.

"Robert, I reviewed the PowerPoint presentation that you sent me on Thursday. It looks pretty good. Christine, do you have any thoughts on it?"

"No, I don't. I think it looks pretty good. On a separate note, I was able to come up with some samples of our work with other clients that will fit with our proposed contact strategy."

"That's great, Christine. Let's see what you've got." Christine laid out the tactical elements on the conference table, including everything from direct mail to telemarketing scripts.

"This looks good," John remarked. "This is going to add a nice touch to our presentation. Thanks for pulling these elements together."

"My pleasure, John."

"Do either of you have any other thoughts that we should discuss before tomorrow," John asked Robert and Christine.

"I do," replied Christine. "I know that I have tomorrow's meeting on my schedule, but what time is it set for?"

"We're meeting at 9:00 A.M. If you'd like, we can all ride over in my car. Considering traffic, we should probably leave here at 8."

"Sounds good, John. Let's all ride together," replied Robert.

"I'll bring coffee for the ride over," said Christine. "How about Starbucks?"

"Sounds good. Thanks for buying, Christine," replied John. "See you all in the morning."

"See you tomorrow," replied Christine and Robert as they left the conference room.

On Monday at 11:00 A.M., the GroupOne team met for their final progress report.

"I hope that you all enjoyed the weather and had a great weekend," said Brian. "I've put together a simple agenda for our meeting tomorrow afternoon. I'll pass around some copies." The agenda mirrored the expectations of Joe Albright. "Wallace, do you want bring up the first slide on the PowerPoint?"

"Sure, Brian."

Brian continued to outline the flow of the presentation.

"Paul, I thought that you might open the presentation with some words of appreciation for our opportunity with AT before stating our agency's mission, vision, and values. I also thought you could share the thoughts and principles that guided your founding of GroupOne, and it would be great if you referenced our work with the residents of New Orleans after Hurricane Katrina. Wallace will have some supporting slides for your introduction. Does that square with what you'd like to present?"

"Yes, it certainly does. I think that what sets us apart from other agencies is our commitment to caring for the community and our tangible support that proves that commitment. With that said, I'll try to spend no more than five to seven minutes on introductory comments."

"That's great, Paul. One more thing: Inasmuch as your presence at the meeting will be a sign of senior management's commitment to AT, I think that actually putting that commitment into words would be helpful."

"Good thought, Brian. I'll make sure I speak on commitment."

Brian continued with the presentation outline. When he got to the point of the strategic and tactical elements that Stephanie and Susan were working on, he and the rest of the team were amazed at the quality of the research. "Stephanie, it's incredible that you were able to devise these high-level process maps and the sample tactics in only a few short days!"

"Thanks, Brian. I think that this will go a long way in communicating the importance of the demand-generation process and, at the same time, provide AT with a taste of the quality planning that we bring to the table."

After spending several minutes reviewing the presentation's closing comments section, Brian wrapped up the meeting by asking if anyone had additional thoughts. When no one responded, Brian ended by addressing Tuesday's schedule. "Since our presentation is set for 2:00 P.M., we should arrive at AT by 1:40. Wallace, were you planning on bringing our LED projector?"

"Yes, I was."

"Great. Joe said that they would have one in the conference room, but I think we should bring ours just in case." After Brian thanked everybody for his or her hard work, the meeting was adjourned.

The team from MarCom Solutions arrived at AT's offices twenty minutes prior to their scheduled meeting time. John Moloney introduced himself to the receptionist who alerted Joe of MarCom's arrival. Joe asked the receptionist to show the group back to the conference room where he was waiting. Joe introduced himself to the team, beginning with John.

"John, pleased to meet you. I'm Joe Albright."

"Joe, it's a pleasure. I'd like you to introduce you to our director of client services, Christine Marquette. And this is Robert Hunte, one of our senior account managers."

Joe shook hands with them. "Pleased to meet both of you."

"Likewise," Christine and Robert replied.

"Please have a seat," Joe continued. "Would any of you like coffee, tea, or water?" "Coffee would be great," John replied, and Christine and Robert requested water.

Joe left the room and quickly returned. As he handed the group their drinks, he said, "Frank and Marlie will be joining us in a few minutes. If you want to take a few minutes to set up, please go a head."

"Thanks, Joe. It'll take just a minute to set up my laptop," John remarked.

Frank and Marlie entered the conference room at 9:00 A.M. sharp. After exchanging introductions with the Scotts, MarCom's team was ready to get started. John took the lead by addressing MarCom's background, vision, mission, and values. After ten minutes of introductory remarks, John turned the presentation over to Robert who presented MarCom's plan recommendations. Christine then took Frank, Marlie, and Joe through some samples of the agency's B2B work, focusing her comments on business issues relevant to AT. Next, John communicated MarCom's unique value proposition. Rambling a bit, he spelled out the value proposition, but failed to portray MarCom as being decidedly "unique."

After John concluded his speech, 25 minutes remained for questions and answers. The Q&A session took 15 minutes. AT's first question concerned MarCom's financial stability, which was followed by questions about the involvement of MarCom's senior management in day-to-day business. John assured Joe and the Scotts that MarCom's founder and president were actively involved and apologized that neither of them were able to be in attendance. Joe brought the meeting to a close by thanking MarCom for their presentation. After exchanging handshakes with Joe and the Scotts, John, Christine, and Robert packed up their materials and headed out the door. Joe and the Scotts stayed behind to discuss their initial impressions.

"Well," Joe asked, "what's your overall impression? Marlie, you first."

"I thought that they appeared competent enough, but I can't say that I was very impressed. On a scale of 1 to 10, I give them a 7."

"Frank, how about you?" Joe asked.

"I'm with Marlie. I thought that the presentation lacked creativity and substance. The preliminary plan recommendations were good, but I didn't see much attention paid to the use of the Internet to help drive qualified leads. MarCom could probably do a sufficient job, but don't we want more than that?"

"Yes, we do," replied Joe. "I was looking for evidence of the work that the agency had performed for other B2B clients and the kind of ROMI that they delivered on those campaigns. The long and short of it is that I'm now more interested than ever to hear what GroupOne has to say."

"I'm with you, Joe," Frank emphasized. "I don't want to be premature in my assessment, but I think that the bar has been set pretty low, and I'll be quite surprised if GroupOne doesn't exceed our expectations."

The team from GroupOne arrived 20 minutes prior to their presentation time. Joe met Brian and the rest of the GroupOne team at the receptionist's counter: "Hi, I'm Brian Walker. You must be Joe Albright."

"That I am," Joe smiled. "Welcome to the offices of Advanced Technologies."

"Joe, I'd like to introduce you to the other members of our team. This is Paul Austin, GroupOne's founder and owner."

Joe reached out to shake Paul's hand. "Paul, it's a pleasure to meet you."

"The feeling is mutual, Joe. Thanks for giving us the opportunity to participate."

Brian went down the line and introduced each person by name and role. Then Joe led the team to the conference room. "Why don't you take a few minutes to settle in, and I'll get everyone some water."

Joe was back in the conference room in a couple of minutes. "Frank and Marlie Scott will be joining us in about five minutes. Brian, were you able to get everything set up?"

"We're fine, Joe. Thanks."

Paul Austin had strategically placed himself at the center of the table so he could watch the nonverbal communication of Joe and the Scotts throughout the presentation. Frank and Marlie entered the conference room at five minutes before the hour. After mutual introductions, Frank took a seat facing the presentation screen. Marlie sat directly to his right. Joe opted for a seat in the midst of GroupOne's team members. To kick things off, Brian stood at the front of the room and thanked the Scotts for the opportunity to present. He introduced GroupOne's team members. Joe introduced AT's senior management and turned the meeting back over to Brian. It was time for Paul to give his introduction.

Standing at the front of the room, Paul began by sharing his gratitude for the opportunity to work with AT and quickly moved on to presenting the specific strategic and tactical recommendations for marketing SecureSoft. The PowerPoint slides that accompanied Paul's remarks hit on the key words of his message, beginning with the background of the agency and how it was founded. Paul's presentation of the vision, mission and values of the organization was brief but significant. GroupOne's stated values were amplified by Paul's stories of how GroupOne made a practice of putting moral principles before business principles. Paul then took the group through a series of slides that addressed GroupOne's gross billings and the specific industries that the agency had worked in, including clients in both the computer hardware and software sectors. As requested, Paul listed the agency's top clients over the past three years and the percentage of agency revenues attributed to each one.

After Paul wrapped up his comments, Wallace kicked off his portion of the presentation by outlining the four key subjects he would be addressing. The first element of his presentation focused on customer relationship development and the customer buying process, which he followed with plan recommendations, the statement of plan objectives, the strategies and tactics of the plan, the time line for implementation and, finally, the line item budget. Wallace closed his presentation by presenting best, probable, and worst case ROI scenarios to quantify expected value.

Stephanie Atwood was up next, presenting three software technology case studies. The programs designed and executed on behalf of the case study clients were multistaged, integrated demand-generation programs. The ROI for each case study was in excess of 300 percent after just six months of program implementation. Stephanie made the point that the value of these programs was generally realized over the long term. Although an enterprise may have a product to sell, prospective customers often lack a need for the product/service at the time it is presented. However, as competitive offerings fail and business conditions change, customer needs change as well, presenting new opportunities. Frank, Marlie and Joe were impressed with the results realized by GroupOne on behalf of their clients.

In closing, Brian Walker gave a final summation of the presentation. As he addressed why AT should select GroupOne over another agency, a text slide entitled "Why GroupOne?" appeared on the screen. "I want to close our presentation by leaving you with three key reasons why GroupOne is the best agency choice for AT and SecureSoft.

1. **Operate with Proven Processes**

    "At GroupOne, we work diligently to create proven processes that are replicable. We begin with the customer in mind and operate within the framework of the customer buying process. We help our B2B clients grow their top line by focusing on the needs, interests, and attitudes of the customer. The results of our multistage, integrated demand-generation solutions speak for themselves. We begin every client relationship with a clear understanding of the business objectives that we are focused on accomplishing. We then put some of the best marketing and sales minds together to design strategies and tactics to achieve those objectives. Finally, with a set of predefined key metrics, we track the performance of these programs and make the necessary course corrections along the way to achieve those objectives."

2. **Proven Track Record**

    Brian continued, "The second reason that we believe we are the right team for AT is that we have a proven track record of performance. We welcome the opportunity to introduce you to several of our clients with whom we've either worked with in the past or continue to work with, because our best spokespeople for the value that we deliver are our clients. Before we leave today, I'll provide you with a list of companies and primary points of contact. I've alerted them that you may be calling, so please take advantage to learn more about the quality of the work that we perform."

3. **Commitment to Serve**

    "Finally," Brian continued, "we are here to serve. Serving our clients, our employees, and the greater good of the community has always been our passion. It would be our pleasure to help AT accomplish its business goals. I trust that we've demonstrated our interest, our capabilities and our commitment to help you achieve your business goals in a way that no other marketing services firm can match. Our thanks to each of you for this opportunity."

Brian then called for questions. Frank Scott's first question came in the form of a "buying signal." "When would you be able to start?" he asked, to which Brian Walker spoke up and said, "Tomorrow."

"Good answer!" Joe exclaimed and then indicated that he, Frank, and Marlie would need to review their notes and follow-up with the provided references. Assuming that AT was able to contact the references in the next couple of days, Joe told GroupOne that they could hear from him as early as Friday. After finishing answering questions, the GroupOne team gathered their materials, said their goodbyes and left the offices of AT.

Frank, Marlie, and Joe stayed in the conference room. Joe asked Frank and Marlie for their impressions.

"This is the right agency, hands down," Frank began. "I still would like you to place the calls to the references, but barring any unusual findings from your calls, this is the agency for us. I'm that impressed."

"I agree," Marlie spoke up. "Let's get those calls made as soon as possible. If all looks as well as it does right now, we have an agency."

Frank turned to Joe. "What do you think?"

"You two said it all," Joe replied. "We've got an agency. I'll start with the calls this afternoon."

"Joe," Frank resumed, "I have to compliment you on the great job you've done in taking us through this process. At the end of the day, the results speak for themselves. I'm very proud of the work we've accomplished."

"Thank you, Frank. And I thank you both for working with me on this journey. Now the fun begins!"

Joe started placing the calls to the client references that afternoon and completed them by mid-day on Wednesday. As expected, the references gave nothing but glowing remarks for the work of GroupOne. After completing the calls, Joe called Frank and Marlie to tell them the results of his calls. A collective decision was made. GroupOne would be AT's new marketing services agency.

Joe first called MarCom Solutions to inform them of AT's decision and spoke briefly with John Moloney. When asked what MarCom could have done better, Joe said that there were many aspects that went into the decision, but that the winning agency's commitment from top management and its proven track record in AT's industry sector was key.

Joe then called Brian Walker. Joe could tell that Brian was ecstatic about the news. After a few minutes of conversation, Joe and Brian agreed to a date and time in the upcoming week for the SecureSoft Agency Kick-Off meeting. After hanging up the phone, Brian sent an IM message to all of GroupOne's employees to announce that there would be a brief meeting at 4:30 P.M. in the company break room.

At 4:30, Brian was in the break room with most of the company staff, including the members of the team that participated in the AT RFP response and presentation. "Everyone, I have some very exciting news to share. But before I do, I'd like to invite Wallace, Susan, Stephanie, and Paul to join me up here. Fellow members of GroupOne," Brian continued, "it is with pride and a sense of accomplishment that I announce that GroupOne has secured a major new client today. The client is Advanced Technologies and the product that we will be focused on helping them market is called SecureSoft. The team before you is the group that made it all happen. From Wallace's outstanding response to the RFP, to Stephanie and Susan's support of Wallace's response, to Paul's continuing vision for GroupOne, I can't begin to tell you how proud I am of our organization. We are a winning team. We are GroupOne."

Epilogue

The story told here is fictional, but the theories, processes, and principles presented are real. Businesses across America and around the globe, both large and small, continue to wrestle with the failure of marketing to align itself with sales and vice versa. Although much has been written on the subject, some of which is referenced in the appendix of this book, opportunity continues to exist to go from talking and thinking about alignment between sales and marketing to actually creating it.

One might ask "Why should I care about aligning sales with marketing?" The answer is as simple as the question. When sales and marketing are in alignment, they work together to more effectively achieve business goals. The marketing team, for example, no longer wastes its time creating "pretty brochures" when research surveys indicate that 90 percent of sales teams never put them to use and that the messages delivered by the sales organization are in concert with the key messages that support the unique value proposition of the company's brand(s).

In my 30-plus years of experience working for Fortune 100 and mid-size companies as a sales and marketing professional, I have seen the value of sales and marketing alignment in action and have worked diligently to create alignment in the organizations that I have served. The process is not difficult, but it takes time and discipline to create lasting change within organizations.

When alignment is realized, an enterprise, its employees, customers, and shareholders become the beneficiaries. There are tools in the appendix of this book that will help get the ball rolling, but, like most major change initiatives in organizations, the place to start is at the top of the organization. Senior management's commitment to creating alignment between sales and marketing will be the key to taking your company's first steps towards more effectively achieving its sales and marketing goals.

Appendix

Elements of Sales & Marketing Alignment

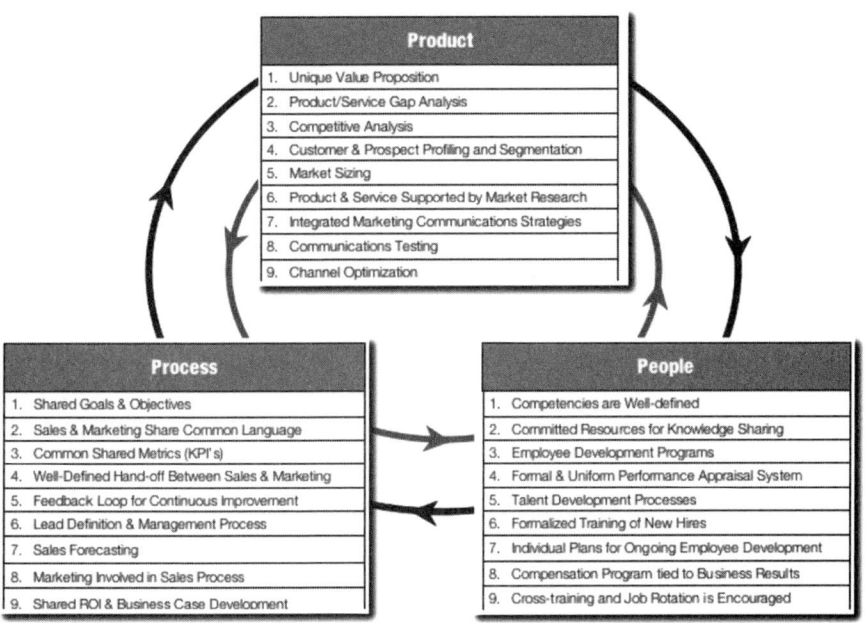

Sales & Marketing Alignment Continuum

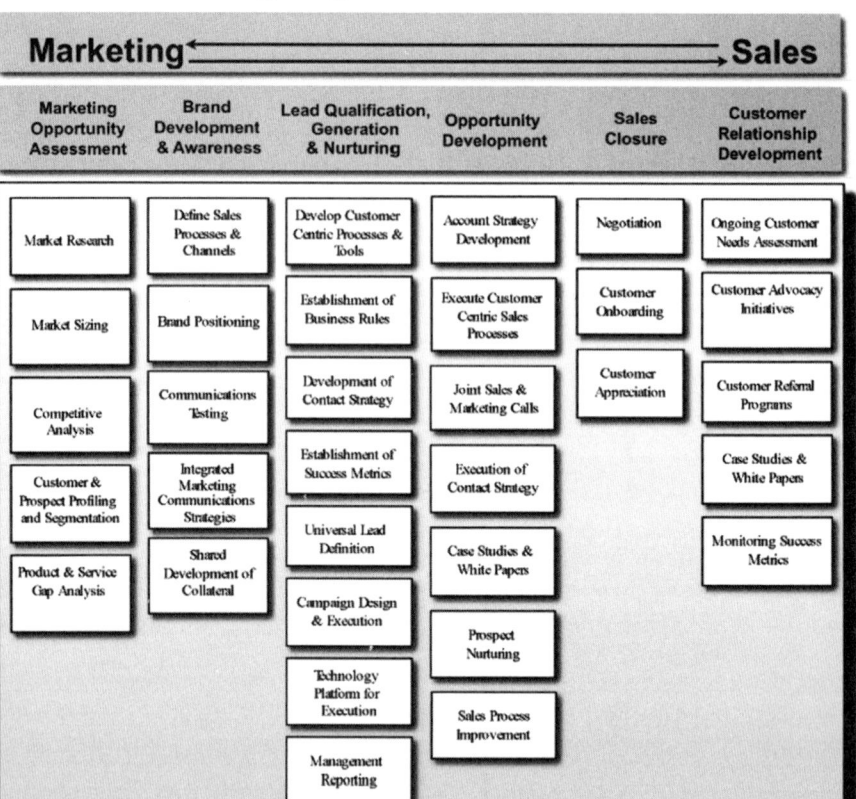

Description of the Sales and Marketing Alignment Continuum

Marketing Opportunity Assessment

Market Research—Qualitative and quantitative research that studies customer issues to arrive at valid prospective solutions.

Market Sizing—Make a list of planning assumptions. Conduct sizing in terms of product/service units/engagements, as well as dollars. Estimate the size of the serviceable/available market (SAM); this is usually no more than 15% of a total market. Then estimate expected company share based on history. Use same methodology for each segment.

Competitive Analysis—Begin with a SWOT analysis. Do the same with competition. Identify competitive strategies. Plot all companies on 2 × 2 matrix.

Customer and Prospect Profiling and Segmentation—Segment the current customer base and identify the various segments that exist based on customer needs. Classify segments by identifying common problems among a group of companies that the company's products/services solve. Each of these segments should value your competitive differential. Identify the common characteristics of and ideal customer for each of these segments. Complete a segmentation profile sheet for each planned segment.

Product & Service Gap Analysis—Based on real and perceived customer needs and the competitive offerings available in the marketplace, this analysis uncovers new opportunities and unmet needs in various customer segments.

Customer Needs Assessment—Assess the needs of the various customer segments relative to the product/service offering of the enterprise. Determine the potential financial benefit for both the customer segments and the enterprise to effectively address this need. This provides management with a gauge to determine the company's current position with respect to satisfying the needs of both current customers and the marketplace at large.

Brand Development & Awareness

Define Sales Processes & Channels—Interviews are conducted with key managers and sales people to determine the best practices and ideal future practices for selling the offering. Channel decisions are based around how the customers buy.

Brand Positioning—Sales-ready messaging is developed to communicate in terms that the buyer understands. Messaging is developed for outgoing marketing communications and for incorporation into the selling process.

Communications Testing—Once the communications strategy has been established, tactical marketing communications are tested with the target audience(s) to assess the ability of the communications to deliver the desired messages and value proposition.

Integrated Marketing Communications Strategies—From web and email to chat and other direct marketing tactics, strategies are assessed and refined to ensure that the communications are reaching the "right" audience at the "right" time with the "right" messages within the "right" marketing communications mediums.

Shared Development of Collateral—Sales and marketing work hand-in-hand to develop marketing and sales collateral materials to ensure that the content and messaging is "customer relevant" and most effective in communicating the value proposition for the company's product and service offering(s).

Lead Qualification, Generation, & Nurturing

Develop Customer-Centric Processes & Tools—Assess and define sales processes to ensure that the focus is customer-centered. Make certain that the point of departure is focused on customer needs/business goals and objectives and how the enterprise's product/service offering may effectively address the customer's goals and objectives.

Establishment of Business Rules—Rules are established to direct the prospect down the appropriate lead management path based on the stage of sales development and size of opportunity.

Development of Contact Strategy—The contact strategy specifies the content, type and frequency of communications that the prospect receives throughout the sales nurturing process.

Establishment of Success Metrics—Identify performance metrics and targets for the product/service of the company. The metrics should be those that accurately assess the performance of the tactics that are being deployed to generate new business through customer acquisition.

Universal Lead Definition—It is critical for sales and marketing to agree in writing on a common definition of the lead. This gives marketing clear direction for developing the marketing plan and provides sales with a definitive hand-off point for developing the sales process to further qualify the lead.

Campaign Design & Execution—Integrated marketing campaign design specifies the objectives of the marketing communications campaign, the targeted segments and the communication elements of the campaign. Once the campaign has been designed, campaign execution and measurement follow.

Technology Platform for Execution and Measurement—Enabling technologies for resource and campaign design and execution, along with technologies required to house and maintain the enterprises' prospect database, is key to supporting new customer acquisition initiatives.

Management Reporting—Define and deliver reporting requirements to monitor and measure the performance of the demand generation and customer acquisition programs.

Opportunity Development

Customer Business Case Development—Develop a cost/benefit model to determine if the value provided by the offering is a good investment of company funds. Also includes planning of sales strategy for key accounts with both sales and marketing teams.

Execute Customer-Centric Sales Processes—Using an SFA tool such as Salesforce.com, monitor results, conduct meetings and coaching sessions, etc., to move prospects through the sales cycle.

Joint Sales & Marketing Calls—Develop guidelines for insertion of marketing personnel into the sales cycle.

Execution of Contact Strategy—Once the contact strategy is specified, execution of the strategy in an effective and quality manner is essential in nurturing both customer and prospect relationships.

Case Studies & White Papers—Case studies and white papers are valuable in pre-sale scenarios to aid in supporting the value proposition of the enterprise, as well as reinforcing the value proposition with post sale customers to aid in developing a climate for up-selling and cross-selling.

Prospect Nurturing—Develop a plan for contacting prospective customers who are not yet ready to enter the sales cycle.

Sales Closure

Negotiation—If necessary, engage in price negotiation. When giving something up, expect something in return.

Customer Onboarding—Implementation of offering post-purchase.

Customer Appreciation—A formal acknowledgement of thanks for the purchase complete with visit/call/letter from top executives and token gifts.

Customer Relationship Development

Ongoing Customer Needs Assessment—Development of a matrix of potential customer needs matched with appropriate company offerings.

Customer Advocacy Initiatives—Customer advocates are an organization's best sales people. Developing mechanisms to help these high-profile/high-value customers "self-identify" is the first step in establishing a high-level customer relationship that the enterprise can leverage in future new customer acquisition programs. For example, campaigns designed to communicate positive customer testimonials to prospective customers has historically paid significant dividends.

Customer Referral Programs—A formal process whereby company sales and management actively seek referrals to other companies/individuals that could prospectively use the company's offerings.

Case Studies & White Papers—Based on performance and success metrics, case studies and white papers are written and published.

Monitoring Success Metrics—Chart actual performance of offering against benchmarks established prior to sale. If results are positive, they form the quantitative basis for success stories or case studies.

Suggested Reading

Articles

Canady, Henry, "A Cool Duo: How to Combine the Best of Both Worlds—Sales & Marketing," Selling Power, Sept., 2007

Kotler, Philip; Rackham, Neal; Krishnaswamy, Suj; MacFarlane, Hugh; Neeson, John, "Ending the War Between Sales& Marketing," Harvard Business Review, Jul., 2006

Neeson, John, "The Sales/Marketing Gap," BtoB Magazine, Jan., 2007

Trailer, Barry; Dickie, Jim, "Understanding What Your Sales Manager is Up Against," Harvard Business Review, Jul., 2006

Anderson, Erin; Onyemah, Vincent, "How Right Should the Customer Be?," Harvard Business Review, Jul., 2006

Books

Bosworth, Michael T.; Holland, John R., *CustomerCentric Selling,* McGraw-Hill, New York, NY, 2004

Carroll, Brian J., *Lead Generation for the Complex Sale,* McGraw-Hill, New York, NY, 2006

Collins, Jim C.; Porras, Jerry I., *Built to Last—Successful Habits of Visionary Companies,* HarperCollins, New York, NY, 1994

Collins, Jim C., *Good to Great,* HarperCollins, New York, NY, 2001

Covey, Steven M.R., *The Speed of Trust,* Free Press, New York, NY, 2006

Creveling, Clive M.; Hambleton, Lynne; McCarthy, Burke, *Six Sigma for Marketing Processes,* Pearson Education, Boston, MA, 2006

Hopkins, Tom, *How to Master the Art of Selling,* Champion Press, Scottsdale, AZ, 1982

MacFarlane, Hugh, *The Leaky Funnel*, MathMarketing, Melbourne, Australia, 2003

Moore, Geoffrey A., *Crossing the Chasm,* HarperCollins, New York, NY, 2002

Peppers, Don; Rogers, Martha, *The One-to-One Future,* Currency Doubleday, New York, NY, 1993

Pyzdek, Thomas, *The Six Sigma Handbook,* McGraw-Hill, New York, NY, 2003

Rackham, Neil, *Spin Selling,* McGraw-Hill, New York, NY, 1988

Rackham, Neil, *How to Ensure Continued Success:Implementation of Account Maintenance Strategies,* McGraw-Hill, New York, NY, 1989

Webb, Michael; Gorman, Tom, *Sales and Marketing the Six Sigma Way,* Kaplan Publishing, Chicago, IL, 2006

Index

A
Advanced Technologies (AT), customer buying process, 51–59
  company needs, 52
  key stakeholders, 53–54
  marketing agency, selection criteria for, 54–55
  sales and marketing needs, steps to satisfy, 52–53
  sales and marketing plan, 56–57
Advanced Technologies (AT), final agency selection
  impression of presentation by GroupOne, 101
  impression of presentation by MarCom Solutions, 98
  selection of GroupOne, 101
Advocacy, 76
Agencies
  researching, 57
  selection criteria for, 54–55
  scorecards for, 54
Agency, collaborative efforts in, 67
Agency presentation, format of, 92

B
Blog, in customer retention program, 75, 76
Brand development/awareness, 69, 107
Brand positioning/awareness, 71
Business profitability, steps to increase, 11–12

C
Case studies, value of, 58, 64–65, 108
CEO, getting buy-in from, 55–56, 93, 95, 99
Client business dynamics, understanding, 49
Closed-loop process, 46, 47, 52
Collins, Jim, 31
Cost/benefit analysis, 39, 40
Critical few, 91
Customer, educating, 53
Customer buying process, 27, *See also Advanced Technology, customer buying process*
Customer-centered philosophy, 74, 75
Customer defection, 73
Customer growth, 75–76
Customer relationship development, 6, 69, 75, 79, 109
Customer retention program, 75, 79

D
Data capture, and privacy, 58
Decision matrix, 91
Demand generation, 71, 72
  impact of, 73–74
  versus lead generation, 66
Demand generation program, 53
Demand generation solution, elements of, 71
Demand generation system, 11
Drucker, Peter, 30

E
Effective communication, characteristics of, 72–73
Enterprise selling process, 27, *See also GroupOne, enterprise selling process*

F
Farming, 26
The Foster Group, 33, 57
  AT evaluation of RFP response, 81, 82, 86, 90

G
GroupOne, company overview, 23–31
  demand generation system at, 28
  marketing team, role of, 28
  performance metrics, 30
  project design/execution at, 29–30
  recruitment and hiring at, 24–27
  sales forecasting at, 28
  sales pipeline at, 28
  selling process at, 27–28
  success principles of, 30–31
GroupOne, enterprise selling process, for Advanced Technologies, 60–69
  case studies, 64–65
  market research, need for, 61–62
  qualitative goals, 61
  quantitative goals, 61
  research, arranging, 64
  RFP planning session, 60–61
  sales and marketing process, outlining, 67
  segmentation research, 62
  strategic business/marketing plan, outlining for client, 65–66
  strategy, execution of, 68–69

GroupOne, response to Advanced
    Technologies (AT) proposal request,
    42–50, 74–75
  AT evaluation of RFP response, 83, 84,
    89, 90
  conference call, with AT consultant, 46–49
  in-house meeting (prior to conference
    call), 45–46
  philosophical approach of, 74
  preliminary work, 56
  preparation for presentation, 94–96, 96–97
  presentation to AT, 98–101
  questions, for AT consultant, 44
  questions, using for competitive
    advantage, 50
  reaction, to winning AT business, 101–2
  research, on AT, 43
  research, on SecureSoft, 43
  RFP, initial review of, 43–44
  seven-step customer buying process, 74–75

H
Hurricane Katrina, 23, 96

I
Industry segments, 34
Internet, in marketing mix, 53
Internet marketing, expertise in, 56, 57, 59

K
Kelvin, William Thompson, 30
Key criteria, in agency selection process, 91
Key managers, compensating, 31
Key metrics, 77
Key performance indicators (KPIs), 11–12,
    77
Keyword search, 57

L
Lead generation, versus demand generation,
    66
Lead qualification/generation/nurturing, 6,
    69, 107–8
Line item estimate, 39
The Lungren Group, 64

M
MarCom Solutions, company overview, 13–22
  client relationships, 16
  client servicing processes, 16
  company services, nature of, 16
  company vision statement, 16
  company work processes, shortcomings
    of, 16, 21
  creative awards programs, 16
  demand generation program, 15
  Internet marketing at, 15, 22
  leadership issues at, 21
  lead generation at, 15
  marketing shortcomings at, 22
  recruitment and hiring at, 13–14
  sales forecasts, 19, 20
  sales pipeline, weakness of, 17, 19
  sales process at, 14–15, 17, 19–21
MarCom Solutions, response to Advanced
    Technologies (AT) proposal request,
    34–40
  AT evaluation of RFP response, 82, 83,
    87, 90, 91
  conference call, with AT consultant, 38–39
  in-house meeting (prior to conference
    call), 34–37
  preparation for presentation, 93–94, 96
  presentation to AT, 97–98
  proposal solution, 39–40
Market, researching, 11, 12
Marketing, role in alignment process, 74
Market opportunity assessment, 6, 69, 106–7
Marketplace opportunity, defining, 70–71
Market research, importance of, 49–50, 61–62
Media habits, of prospects, 72, 73
Multichannel, 61
Multistage, 61

O
Obstacles, to goal achievement, 46
Opportunity development, 69, 108–9

P
Pareto principle, 14
Periodic communication, 71–72
Planning/process design, in alignment
    process, 76
PracticeOne, 28–30
  key metrics for, 29
  statistics for, 29–30
President, getting buy-in from, 55–56, 93,
    95, 99
Pricing model, 4
Primary needs, identifying, 46
Primary research, 34
  to define brand position, 71
  to define market opportunity, 70
Product benefits, 4
Product characteristics, 4
Product pricing, 4
Profiling, 106
  to quantify customer value, 79
Prospect nurturing, 72–73, 74, 109
Prospect universe, determining, 34

Q

Qualified lead, defining, 6, 28, 66
Qualitative research, 61, 63
Quantitative research, 34, 61, 63
Questions, for businesses to consider, 44

R

Request for proposal (RFP), response framework, 78–79
RFP responses, evaluation of
  by company owners, 86–87
  by consultant, 80–84
  joint assessments, 87–90
Return on marketing investment (ROMI), 40, 41
Return on investment (ROI), 40, 41
"Right" people, importance of, 31

S

SaaS, 4, 28, 43
SaaS providers, 28
Sales, forecasting, 11
Sales and marketing, interrelationship of, 67, 68
Sales and marketing alignment
  benefits of, 103
  HR requirements of, 7
Sales and marketing alignment, process for, 70–79
  advocacy, 76
  brand positioning/awareness, 71
  customer growth, 75–76
  customer relationship development, 75, 79
  customer retention, 75, 79
  demand generation, 71–72, 74
  marketplace opportunity, 70–71
  planning/process design, 76
  process, refining, 77
  processes, implementing, 77
  program, measuring, 77
  prospect nurturing, 72–73, 74
  sales opportunity development, 74–75
Sales and marketing alignment, steps in, 76–77
  execution, 77
  measurement, 77
  planning/process design, 76
  refinement, 77
Sales and marketing alignment continuum, 106–9
Sales and marketing alignment model, 6–7
Sales and marketing plan, 5–6
Sales and marketing processes, implementing, 77
Sales budget, 5
Sales closure, 69, 109
Sales cycle, 4
Sales opportunity development, 74–75
Sales process, developing, 14–15, 17
Scorecard, 59
  in RFP responses, 80
Search engines, company presence in, 57, 58, 59
Secondary research, 34
SecureSoft, 1, 2
  benefits of, 4
  characteristics of, 4
  pricing, 4
  prospective users of, 34
  RFP, to prospective agency partners, 32, 33
  sales budget for, 5
  sales cycle, 4
  sales plan for, preparing, 33–34
  SWOT review, 8
  unique value proposition of, 8, 10
  ways to assess/improve, 75, 76
Segmentation, 106
  to quantify customer value, 79
Segmentation research, 62
Selection criteria, for agencies, weighting, 55
Senior management, and commitment to alignment, 103
Senior sales executive, recruiting, 85, 87, 89, 93
Service, commitment to, 23, 24, 31
Six Sigma DMAIC process, 77, 79
Slone Direct, 33, 57
  AT evaluation of RFP response, 80, 81, 86, 90
Social media strategy, 59
Software Solutions, Inc., 28–30
Stakeholders, in buying/selling process, 53–54
Strategic business/marketing plan, outlining for client, 65–66
Strategy, execution of, 68–69
SWOT analysis, 2–3, 8

T

Top talent, retaining, 31

U

Unique value proposition (UVP), 8
User group, in customer retention program, 75

V

Value, versus cost, 38, 39, 40

W

Web presence, value of, 56
White papers, value of, 58, 108

Racom Communications Order Form

QUANTITY	TITLE	PRICE	AMOUNT
_____	Contemporary Direct and Interactive Marketing, 3rd Ed., **Spiller/Baier**	$69.95	_____
_____	The *IMC Handbook*, **J. Stephen Kelly/Susan K. Jones**	$49.95	_____
_____	*Creative Strategy in Direct & Interactive Marketing, 4th Ed.*, **Susan K. Jones**	$49.95	_____
_____	*Innovating . . . Chcago Style*, **Thomas Kuczmarski, Luke Tanen, Dan Miller**	$27.95	_____
_____	*The New Media Driver's License*, **Richard Cole/Derek Mehraban**	$24.95	_____
_____	*Aligned*, **Maurice Parisien**	$19.95	_____
_____	*How to Jump-Start Your Career*, **Robert L. Hemmings**	$19.95	_____
_____	*This Year a Pogo Stick . . . Next Year a Unicycle!*, **Jim Kobs**	$19.95	_____
_____	*Follow That Customer*, **Egbert Jan van Bel/Ed Sander/Alan Weber**	$39.95	_____
_____	*Internet Marketing*, **Herschell Gordon Lewis**	$19.95	_____
_____	*Reliability Rules*, **Don Schultz/Reg Price**	$34.95	_____
_____	*The Marketing Performance Measurement Toolkit*, **David M. Raab**	$39.95	_____
_____	*Successful E-Mail Marketing Strategies*, **Arthur M. Hughes/Arthur Sweetser**	$49.95	_____
_____	*Managing Your Business Data*, **Theresa Kushner/Maria Villar**	$32.95	_____
_____	*Media Strategy and Planning Workbook*, **DL Dickinson**	$24.95	_____
_____	*Marketing Metrics in Action*, **Laura Patterson**	$24.95	_____
_____	*Print Matters*, **Randall Hines/Robert Lauterborn**	$27.95	_____
_____	*The Business of Database Marketing*, **Richard N. Tooker**	$49.95	_____
_____	*Customer Churn, Retention, and Profitability*, **Arthur Middleton Hughes**	$44.95	_____
_____	*Data-Driven Business Models*, **Alan Weber**	$49.95	_____
_____	*Branding Iron*, **Charlie Hughes and William Jeanes**	$27.95	_____
_____	*Managing Sales Leads* and *Sales & Marketing 365*, **James Obermayer**	$56.95	_____
_____	*Creating the Marketing Experience*, **Joe Marconi**	$49.95	_____
_____	*Coming to Concurrence*, **J. Walker Smith/Ann Clurman/Craig Wood**	$34.95	_____
_____	*Brand Babble*, **Don E. Schultz/Heidi F. Schultz**	$24.95	_____
_____	*The New Marketing Conversation*, **Donna Baier Stein/Alexandra MacAaron**	$34.95	_____
_____	*Trade Show and Event Marketing*, **Ruth Stevens**	$59.95	_____
_____	*Accountable Marketing*, **Peter J. Rosenwald**	$59.95	_____
_____	*Contemporary Database Marketing*, **Martin Baier/Kurtis Ruf/G. Chakraborty**	$89.95	_____
_____	*Catalog Strategist's Toolkit*, **Katie Muldoon**	$59.95	_____
_____	*Marketing Convergence*, **Susan K. Jones/Ted Spiegel**	$34.95	_____
_____	*High-Performance Interactive Marketing*, **Christopher Ryan**	$39.95	_____
_____	*Public Relations: The Complete Guide*, **Joe Marconi**	$49.95	_____
_____	*The Marketer's Guide to Public Relations*, **Thomas L. Harris/Patricia T. Whalen**	$39.95	_____
_____	*The White Paper Marketing Handbook*, **Robert W. Bly**	$39.95	_____
_____	*Business-to-Business Marketing Research*, **Martin Block/Tamara Block**	$69.95	_____
_____	*Hot Appeals or Burnt Offerings*, **Herschell Gordon Lewis**	$24.95	_____
_____	*On the Art of Writing Copy*, **Herschell Gordon Lewis**	$39.95	_____
_____	*Open Me Now*, **Herschell Gordon Lewis**	$21.95	_____
_____	*Marketing Mayhem*, **Herschell Gordon Lewis**	$39.95	_____
_____	*Asinine Advertising*, **Herschell Gordon Lewis**	$22.95	_____
_____	*The Ultimate Guide To Purchasing Website, Video, Print & Other Creative Services*, **Bobbi Balderman**	$18.95	_____

Name/Title _____

Company _____

Street Address _____

City/State/Zip _____

Email _____ Phone _____

Credit Card: ☐ VISA ☐ MasterCard
              ☐ American Express ☐ Discover

☐ Check or money order enclosed (payable to Racom Communications in US dollars drawn on a US bank)

Number _____ Exp. Date _____

Signature _____

Subtotal _____

Subtotal from other side _____

8.65% Tax _____

Shipping & Handling _____
$7.00 for first book; $1.00 for each additional book.

TOTAL _____

Racom Communications, 150 N. Michigan Ave, Suite 2800, Chicago, IL 60601
312-494-0100, 800-247-6553, www. Racombooks.com